"Gina Mollicone-Long walks the walk, not just talks the talk. Her clarity and confidence jump off the page and into my mind and heart."

— Charmaine Crooks, Five-Time Olympian (Athletics), Silver Medalist

"This book is a winner. It's an insightful, inspirational and practical guide to getting the most out of your life. Gina reclaims the idea of failure, and almost makes it appealing."

— Bruce Sellery, Host, Workopolis TV, Report on Business Television

"Gina Mollicone-Long has devised a new way to understand and squeeze value from the adventure we call life. Backed by the wise counsel of the ages and her own unique insights, we discover that the ability to grasp and exploit failure may be the greatest life-skill of all."

— Robert Genn, www.painterskeys.com

"I had heard some of these ideas before, but I've never seen them presented in a way that I felt I could actually integrate them into the way I think and live. This is a life-changing book."

— Dr. Janet Taylor, Psychiatrist

"Gina is a woman who grabs you instantly with her massive intellect and holds you forever enamoured because of her even bigger heart. If the world were in her hands we could all breathe a huge sigh of relief. Her book takes a highly emotional and often frustrating subject and guides you compassionately yet effectively through to understanding how you can finally claim your outstanding life. Read it and learn."

— Alexandra Watson, Happiness Expert and Best-Selling Author of *The Happiness System for Women*

"A must-read. The book flips a switch in your brain. Gina takes that 'niggling feeling' you've always had and shows you how to use it to get what you want. Her generosity sets this book apart, allowing one to hear things in a way they haven't heard before, and therefore do things they may have never done before."

— Kim Parlee, Host & Anchor, Report on Business Television

"Gina Mollicone-Long has perfected the art of the successful journey—one dotted with tools, lessons and the secrets to the fulfillment of our individual dreams and desires. A magnificent blueprint for how to tap into our existing and future resources."

— Sara Genn, Artist

"What if we considered not getting what we want a gift instead of a disappointment? This challenge to our perceptual norms is the heart of The Secret of Successful Failing. Gina Mollicone-Long brings her fierce passion, bright enthusiasm and infectious energy to uncovering all the cognitive threads around this alternative path to true success."

—Karen Schaffer, Career Coach & Author of *The Job of Your Life* and *The Complete Book of Resumes*

"It's funny, but when we think of the people whom society deems 'successful,' it's easy to see how obstacles were a natural part of their journey. And yet when it's our own journey, too often we throw in the towel the first time we hit so much as a pothole. 'Oh well, guess it wasn't meant to be!' Mollicone-Long calls us on our 'b-s' as only she can, reminding us that those bumps along the way aren't setbacks, but rather our rites of passage."

—Mary-Jo Dionne, Writer, Comedian

"When Gina Mollicone-Long writes, the profound becomes simple and the cosmic proves to be universal reality. Anyone who wants to develop greater awareness in their relationships with themselves and others should read this book. Gina's enthusiasm for life and the betterment of humanity shines through in an easy-to-read and inspiring format."

—Gianna Piccardo, Balanced Wellness Yoga & Ayurvedic Therapy

"A refreshing approach to why and how we should follow our heart, not our head. My favorite is 'You Can't Fix Your Hair by Combing the Mirror.'"

—Dr. Bill Code, MD, Author of *Winning the Pain Game*

"Beautifully done! This is a must-read for anyone who has said, 'I've tried everything!' Try this and change your life!"

—Ann McIndoo, Author of *So, You Want to Write!*

"Gina helps you learn how to fail successfully. If you can learn this critical skill, you can accomplish anything."

—Paige Kearin, Motivational Speaker & Author

"This is one of the most inspiring books I have read. Gina keeps you on the edge of your seat wanting to read more. It is like having your very own private conversation with her, as she shares personal experiences and motivates you into embracing your failures…that is the secret, the answer to happier living. 'The content of the book comes from a sacred space within me,' she writes, and it is written with honesty and sincerity. It will inspire you and make a positive difference in your life. Thank you, Gina Mollicone-Long. You have made a difference."

—Linda Lane, Project Officer, Government of Ontario

THE SECRET OF SUCCESSFUL FAILING

THE SECRET OF
SUCCESSFUL
FAILING

Hidden inside every failure is exactly
what you need to get what you want

GINA MOLLICONE-LONG

))((Pathfinders
))PUBLISHING

Toronto, ON, Canada
Seattle, WA, USA

Pathfinders Publishing
36 Toronto Street, Suite 850
Toronto, Ontario, Canada, M5C 2C5
PH: (877) 901-9298
FAX: (905) 844-8153
www.pathpub.com
orders@pathpub.com

Pathfinders Publishing
999 3rd Avenue, Suite 3800
Seattle, WA 98104 USA
PH: (877) 901-9298
FAX: (905) 844-8153
www.pathpub.com
orders@pathpub.com

This publication is designed to educate and provide general information regarding the subject matter covered. It is not intended to replace the counsel of other professional advisors. The reader is encouraged to consult with his or her own advisors regarding specific situations. While the author has taken reasonable precautions in the preparation of this book and believes the facts presented within the book are accurate, neither the publisher nor author assumes any responsibility for errors or omissions. The author and publisher specifically disclaim any liability resulting from the use or application of the information contained in this book. The information within this book is not intended to serve as emotional or therapeutic advice related to individual situations.

Printed in the United States of America on 100% PCW Recycled, Acid Free and Elementally Chlorine Free Paper. 79 trees and many other resources were saved as a result. Learn more at www.greenpressinitiative.org.

Library and Archives Canada Cataloguing in Publication

Mollicone-Long, Gina, 1970-
    The secret of successful failing : hidden inside every failure is exactly what you need to get what you want / Gina Mollicone-Long.

ISBN 978-0-9782415-0-6

    1. Failure (Psychology) 2. Success. I. Title.
BF575.F14M64 2007   158.1   C2007-900141-6
PCCN 2007920090

Editing: Brookes Nohlgren and Andrew Long
Cover and book design: Patricia Bacall

dedication

"Miracles occur naturally as expressions of love.
The real miracle is the love that inspires them.
In this sense everything that comes
from love is a miracle."

—Marianne Williamson

This book is dedicated to two
very important people in my life
whom I love very much.
First, to Andrew, for believing in me
and inspiring me to start this book.
Second, to Roxolana,
for inspiring me to finish it.

table of contents

	Acknowledgements	xi
	Preface	xvii
Chapter 1	Failure Is the Fast Track to Success	1
Chapter 2	The Feedback Loop of Life	25
Chapter 3	BE – The Energetic Reality	49
Chapter 4	DO – The Temporary Reality	75
Chapter 5	HAVE – The Physical Reality	97
Chapter 6	Things That Help	117
Chapter 7	Things That Don't	141
Chapter 8	The Life of *Your* Dreams	161
Chapter 9	The 42 Things That Will Positively Change Your Life	181
Appendix	Book Club Discussions	191

acknowledgements

*"At times our own light goes out and
is rekindled by a spark from another person.
Each of us has cause to think with deep gratitude
of those who have lighted the flame within us."*
—Albert Schweitzer

I have often pondered how many people were truly involved in helping me write this book. People often think of the obvious supporters, but they rarely consider just how many people have inspired a thought, an idea, or a concept. I have thought about this a lot because I want all of these people to understand how truly grateful I am for their contribution. Since this is my first book the list is long, but it is not even wholly complete. It is the best effort I could make at acknowledging the immense support I have experienced from people and the Universe in creating this book. Thank you from the bottom of my heart to everyone who has been a part of this process. If I have managed to overlook anyone, please accept my apologies and know that a place of gratitude exists for you in my heart.

First and foremost, I want to thank my children, Molly and Simon, for allowing their mommy the time and space to create this book. I cherish their ability to accurately reflect my exact emotional state with ease. I would be nowhere without them.

Next, I would like to thank those who were instrumental in helping me complete this project, namely my staff, including Jen Caldwell, Elise Vos, Ashley Audet and Flo Shi. I would like to thank Ellen Reid for shepherding me to the brilliant team of editor, Brookes Nohlgren; copywriter, Laren Bright; and designer, Patricia Dacall. I would also like to thank Professor Will Cluett at the University of Toronto for helping to fill in my memory gaps about feedback loops from my days in chemical engineering. Drew Nederpelt has been generous with his industry insight. Finally, I would like to thank Ann McIndoo for helping me to get started with the first verbal draft.

I would also like to thank the following people for being a fundamental part of who I am—without them, I would never have been able to accomplish much. My parents, Jane Panasik and Mario Mollicone, for the obvious ways they have made me who I am. My grandparents for their links to my history. To my sister, Marla, for being one of the early adopters of some of my out-of-the-mainstream approaches, and to my brother, Dan, especially for his ability to explain things such as quantum theory with ease. Thank you, too, to my best childhood friends, Joanne VidAmour and Angie LaFontaine, for being there like sisters for all those years when I was finding my voice. Thank you to Andrew Cizek, who has been somewhere between big brother and cousin.

Additionally, I would like to thank a special group of women who have been immensely supportive. To MJ Dionne, Annabel Varvel, Kathy Kortes-Miller and Sara Genn for reading the initial versions of the book. My oh my, how it has changed since then. I would also like to acknowledge the support and friendship of the women in my PowHERpod, including Gianna Piccardo, Jane Roos, Paige Kearin, Alex Watson, Maritza Parra, Luz Parra and Fabiana Bacchini. I am particularly grateful to my "Bowen Island Girls," Titania Michniewicz, Laura Ruloff and Jennifer Hansen, for being a huge part of my reawakening. Titania especially for your clarity with the cards. I also wish to thank my amazing girlfriends from my Vancouver days, including Christina deHaas, Erin Roux, Lori McIntosh, Michèle Daignault and Diane Dol, for putting up with my constant barrage of book ideas. I told you I would get one out at some point. These women know how many book ideas I still have in me! Where would I be without my "Triumvirate Girls," Shelley Van-Sickle and Roxolana Buckle? Thank you for always being there for me. Finally, a special thank you to some young women who have had taught me a lot more about life than they will ever know, including Alana Diebel, Amy Adams, Alicia Hoppenrath and the entire Dunbar Jaguars Soccer Team.

I would also like to acknowledge the following people, who most likely have no idea that they provided necessary inspiration, information or motivation for this book. Usually, it was a profound conversation or interaction that guided me in this project. First, to Lynda and Ed Long for having a cottage in such

a beautiful place that I was inspired to finally put these words on paper. Famous artists have used this same location to create timeless pieces, and I borrowed from their creative energy. I would also like to thank Melissa Doyle, Trish Long, Al Lysne, Jane Roos, Conrad Leinemann, Dave Lotocki, Bob Panasik, Chris Holliday, Tracy White, Fran McAleer, Jeff Roux, Kristine, Ed & Mary Drakich, Andrew Kaye, Andrea Cuthbert, Kim Parlee, Elizabeth Jarosz, Bruce Sellery and my coaching clients for allowing me to voice my ideas, theories and concepts and for challenging me to be a better person. A special thanks to Andrea Gray for inspiring the life-changing marathon.

There are a whole host of people who have been supportive behind the scenes. The following people have contributed their technical expertise. First to Heather Kenalty for being able to capture my energy in a photograph. Next to the web designer extraordinaire, Ryan Strom. Finally, to Lucy and Jon Barber who have registered and supported as many URLs as I have ideas. There are also many gifted healers and alternative health providers who have supported or continue to support me in my "human-ness" on a physical, emotional and spiritual level. Thank you to Janice Hall, Miriam Erlichman, Andrea Bartliff, Chris Lacey, Mary McDonagh, Catherine Shaw and Karen Hood-Caddy.

An honourable mention should definitely go to God, the Creator, the Universe, for bestowing upon me my gifts and the ability to express them. For this I am truly blessed and eternally grateful.

Last but definitely not least, I want to thank my husband, soulmate and best friend, Andrew. Andrew's unwavering support and belief in my abilities is astounding. He truly reflects my most powerful qualities, and for this I am immensely grateful. His ability to see the greatness and disregard the rest has been a major impetus in finishing this project. He has done more than his fair share of parenting over the last few years—and he has done it joyfully and without complaint. He may not think I notice, but I do. He is also one hell of a thorough yet compassionate editor. There is no way in the world I could have pulled this off without him.

I HOPE YOU DANCE

Words and Music by Tia Sillers and Mark D. Sanders

I hope you never lose your sense of wonder,
You get your fill to eat but always keep that hunger,
May you never take one single breath for granted,
God forbid love ever leave you empty handed,
I hope you still feel small when you stand beside the ocean,
Whenever one door closes I hope one more opens,
Promise me that you'll give faith a fighting chance,
And when you get the choice to sit it out or dance.

I hope you dance...I hope you dance.

I hope you never fear those mountains in the distance,
Never settle for the path of least resistance
Livin' might mean takin' chances but they're worth takin',
Lovin' might be a mistake but it's worth makin',
Don't let some hell bent heart leave you bitter,
When you come close to sellin' out reconsider,
Give the heavens above more than just a passing glance,
And when you get the choice to sit it out or dance.

Dance....I hope you dance.

preface

"Our greatest glory is not in never falling,
but in rising every time we fall."

—Confucius

I must begin by emphasizing that this book is based on my experience and mine alone. My intention in writing it is to make a positive contribution to others by sharing my story and what I have learned. My unwavering desire is to make this world a better place. I am not attempting to present my knowledge as the one and only "truth," so please don't take it that way. If the ideas and concepts in this book make your life easier, then by all means use them. On the other hand, if any ideas offered here do not work for you, then please disregard them and keep reading.

I recognize that some people will not agree with what I have written. I allow for this. I also know that some people will have trouble with the concepts presented here. I allow for this also. The book contains spiritual references that may be a source of difficulty for some. I respect that each of us experiences divinity in a unique way, or not at all. The spiritual references made here represent *my* experience of

divinity. Please feel free to insert your own terminology for expressing the concept of the Universe, God, Infinite Wisdom or otherwise. As noted, this book is not intended to be the "truth" but rather my interpretation of my own life experiences.

I have had many teachers along my path. I am truly grateful for everything they have taught me. Many of the materials, concepts and ideas in this book are as old as time. This book is an attempt to explain them through the eyes of my experience. I believe that we have all come here to make a contribution to the world. This book is part of my contribution. I hope that you will have at least one, if not many, "a-ha" moments while reading it.

I still can't believe that I have written a self-help book using the education I gained while studying chemical engineering at the University of Toronto. It is a great illustration of "trusting the process" even though I couldn't really see the whole picture. I had no idea how important feedback loops would be when I wrote my thesis back in 1993. Thank Heavens I was paying attention in that class and that I maintained connections to UofT so I could go back and clarify the things I had forgotten. They say that hindsight is always 20/20 and now this all makes sense to me.

My ultimate hope is that this book helps you see your life as perfect *right now*, exactly as it is—that you stop looking for what's wrong and start seeing the beauty that is right in front of you. Remember, you have attracted this book into your hands right now for a reason. There are thousands of

other books on the shelves, yet you are holding this one. Perhaps there is a sentence in this book written just for you.

The ideas that fill this book have worked (and continue to work) for me. My life is by no means perfect, but it is rich with experience. I am not much different from you. I still have "those days" as well. However, I am committed to reducing their power over my happiness by using the tools written about here. The content of this book comes from a sacred space within me and I have decided to share it with you so that it may inspire you, too. My sincere wish is that it makes a positive difference in your life.

I hope you dance!

"Life must be understood backward.
But it must be lived forward."

—Soren Kierkegaard

chapter 1

FAILURE IS THE FAST TRACK TO SUCCESS

"The world is round, and the place which may seem like the end may also be the beginning."

—Ivy Baker Priest

If you are wondering why on earth you would want to read a book that starts by saying that failure is the fast track to success, please consider yourself normal. The paradox is astounding, if you pay attention. Consider that most of the time, for most of us anyway, we don't get exactly what we want. And most of the time we are disappointed about NOT getting what we want. Consider also that we spend very little of our time being happy because our happiness is conditional upon getting what we want. No "get" equals no "happy." Does this sound at all familiar?

What if you could turn this around? What if you could experience NOT getting what you want and still feel happy? What if you could start to see that NOT getting what you want is a good thing? What if you could be happy regardless of what is happening to you? Would you want to know

how to do it? Excellent! That's where we begin. This will be your step-by-step guide to turning those times of seeming powerlessness and disappointment into sources of strength, happiness and growth.

You Can't Fix Your Hair by Combing the Mirror

When we look in a mirror, we see ourselves reflected. It seems silly, doesn't it, to blame the mirror if we don't like what we see? Doesn't it also seem silly to try to somehow modify the mirror to get a different picture? On the contrary, in order to change the image being reflected, we need to change *ourselves*. In other words, if we don't like the results we get in life, it's futile to blame the results themselves or our circumstances. To see different results, we must make a change *inside of us*. This, and only this, will create a different reflection in the mirror.

This book is a different kick at a familiar can. Throughout the ages, people have searched for the path to happiness and for ways to get what they want. Thousands and thousands of books and systems have been written or designed to help us get what we want. Yet, still, most of the time we don't get what we want and are left with a sense of failure or un-fulfillment.

Most of us have learned to be disappointed by failure. We have been conditioned to believe that failure causes pain and therefore should be avoided at all costs—even if those costs include happiness, self-expression and joy. Our

conditioning has not allowed us to view failure as an opportunity for learning. We have never been taught how to use our failure to attract everything we've ever wanted. We have never been taught to view failure as what it really is—our greatest building block—so that it can become the most positive force in accelerating us towards living the lives of our dreams. Our failures hold the key to what is standing between us and everything our hearts desire. The answers are right in front of us if we choose to see them. However, we have been conditioned to focus on avoiding failure rather than learning from it. We spend countless hours analyzing WHY we failed instead of analyzing HOW our failure can help us. We focus on the obstacle instead of the solution, on the outside instead of the inside.

The path to happiness lies in seeing each failure as a signpost along the journey of life. These signposts give us valuable feedback about what is really happening to us on the inside. If we pay attention to what we are seeing, we will finally begin to make powerful life choices.

Happiness Is a Choice

Throughout our entire lives we have been conditioned to believe that in order to be happy we have to get *something*, be it fame, fortune, beauty or even spirituality. We have been continually told that the answer to our happiness lies "out there." WRONG! Happiness is a choice. If we are not happy, then we have chosen it that

We have the power within us to be happy, no matter
is happening *to* us. We have been trained to abdi-
this power to something beyond our control and
been conditioned to wait, hope and even pray for
thing to change on the outside so that we can finally
ppy on the inside. Our lives merely reflect the
es we have made about ourselves. If we want to see
hing different in our lives, we first have to make a
ent choice.

other problem is that we want happiness in all
nts of life, but we don't see the wisdom that can
hrough unhappiness. We haven't been taught to see
happiness of life as "perfect" and exactly what we
o get where we're going. We haven't been taught
learn our lessons along the way and to deal with
l emotions that accompany them. Instead, we've
ught over and over again that we must avoid being
by and must continue to repress this feeling with
lty logic that if we avoid being unhappy, by default
be happy. WRONG again! Numb doesn't equal
Besides, by focusing on not being unhappy we can
attract more unhappiness into our lives. I'll explain
this in great detail in the upcoming chapters, but it's true
because we always attract what we focus on. Remember,
happiness is a choice. In order to choose happiness, we
have to first be aware of our power to choose, and then
regularly and consistently make that choice.

This is why NOT getting what you want is such a gift. If you allow yourself to really experience what is happening to you, then you finally open up to receive the full extent of what you want. When you trust in the wisdom of the Universe, begin to see your failures as useful and embrace their teaching, then you are able to move through obstacles and achieve true happiness. You will be able to see the real results of your choices, thus allowing you to finally choose something different.

Think about it for a minute: You weren't always afraid of failure. In fact, there was a time in your life when you were free to experience the fullness of life. A time when you approached life with reckless abandon and tried things simply for the pleasure of that moment. Children possess an uncanny knack for living in the moment, for experiencing real life with its ups and downs. They seem to have a magic formula for dealing with anything that gets dealt to them. If you've ever observed a child, then you know that they experience life in real time, processing emotions as the feelings come and letting them go just as easily. They aren't attached to anything. They don't avoid failure, plan their escape route or take the safest path. They just live and deal with life as it comes. Have you ever seen a toddler go from extreme bliss to utter devastation, back to extreme bliss—in

> *"Failure is just another way to learn how to do something right."*
> —Marian Wright Edelman

under three minutes? This is what I am talking about. They don't hold on to anything or censor anything or run in the opposite direction of anything. Children are the greatest teachers we could ever have. Right in front of us. Being free.

Learned Behaviours

Children don't get stuck in their failures, but they do experience the emotions associated with them in real time. They cry, throw tantrums, hit, kick and scream in the present moment. And then they learn. They learn from us what is appropriate, what is expected and what is "right." They learn that it is somehow not okay to cry. They learn that it is somehow not okay to feel what they are feeling in the present moment. They are scolded, ridiculed, shamed and even ignored. They begin to question themselves and they learn to avoid feeling certain emotions because that's easier than trying to explain them, manage them or suppress them. Because failure often leads to these intense emotions, children learn to avoid failure—and in avoiding failure, they stop taking risks.

I'm sure you can see where I am going with this. Most of us learned to stop living the life of our dreams because it was too risky to manage all of that emotion in a world that wouldn't allow it. We learned to stop reaching for the stars because the risk of failure far outweighed the probability of success. We learned this from someone else. The good news is that we can UNlearn it too!

Safety

A word about why this happens. The human mind is always trying to plan life so that it's safe. Predictable means safe because we can guess the outcome. A very basic brain function is to keep us alive, to keep the sabretoothed tigers away! Having a brain actually gives us an advantage in the survival game because we are able to predict the outcome. The mind is always trying to predict, predict, predict—it is a prediction machine. The mind is always asking, "Is this going to be safe?" This is an inherent design flaw in the human being. But while the mind's purpose is to be safe, the heart's purpose is to be free. You can plainly see how these two agendas conflict. We feel this conflict when we want to do something but our internal alarm system goes ballistic, saying, "No! Stop! Not safe! Not safe! Danger! Unpredictable!"

This is exactly what happened when we learned that failure was risky business, because shame and ridicule usually followed. The mind quickly caught on that it could predict just how much shame and ridicule lay ahead by the size of the quest that the heart wanted to undertake. As we got older, our prediction machine got better and better at keeping us in a safety zone where it could easily predict the outcome. As a result, our ability to reach for the stars vanished because our minds were consumed with keeping us safe. It is interesting to observe that as we age, our comfort zone gets smaller and smaller yet our discontent grows larger

and larger. Hmmm, maybe there is a connection! Perhaps all this discontent is the result of living half a life, a safe life, a life with no risks and therefore no rewards. Call me crazy, but I think that's what has happened. As they say, "The first step to solving a problem is recognition of the problem." By the way, for those of you who are saying, "This is nonsense," I just want to remind you that that's your mind talking as it desperately tries to keep you safe! And it's a sure-fire sign that you need to step out of your comfort zone right now. Just keep reading and I'll explain all of it in more detail.

The only person you can be is yourself. The only person I can be is myself. When we try to be someone else, trouble arises. If an artist is trapped in an accountant's life or vice versa, then she is not being true to herself. She probably has a lot of anxiety because she is split off from her true self. She is split off from her higher purpose. I suggest that the angst in her life doesn't come from getting or not getting things she wants; it actually comes from being split off from her purpose—her true self. This split occurred when she realized that it wasn't okay to be herself. This split will keep presenting itself in our "mirror" over and over again in many different circumstances until we finally get the message and see the reflection for what it is.

Cosmic Two-by-Fours

Oprah once said, "God first speaks to us in whispers." The key to getting the message is to listen for it. However,

if we miss the first message from God, then it comes a little louder the next time and keeps getting louder until She finally cracks us with a "cosmic two-by-four" to make sure we are paying attention. This has happened to me many, many times, but a particularly significant "cosmic two-by-four" was the one that hit me before starting this book. I was desperately trying to "shove a square peg into a round hole" (as I often do) when I got so frustrated that I blurted out, "Why don't I ever get what I want?" I was so angry that life was so hard all the time. Then, it hit me—hard! I was screaming at the mirror. I was desperately trying to change the outside world so it wouldn't make me mad anymore. Then I got it. I finally understood that everything I experience is a reflection of me. If I wanted to see a different reflection, then I had to change *on the inside*. This was a huge gift, even though it took a cosmic two-by-four to get me there.

You are what you say you are. It's a choice you make. You may have decided to make that choice based on what someone else said to you, but the bottom line is that you have chosen it this way. You act according to what you believe or say. Each person is unique with her or his own purpose for being on this earth. I know that sounds a bit simple or trite, but it is paramount to appreciating who you really are. Each person on this earth has come with a higher purpose. Every single purpose, like every single snowflake, is different. Our responsibility is not only to

ourselves, but also to all of the other people on Earth. We already know how much we ourselves suffer when we don't live our true life, but we need to recognize that the rest of the universe also suffers because of it—because everyone else is also being robbed of the difference we could be making in the world.

> "Our deepest fear is not that we are inadequate. Our deepest fear is that we are powerful beyond measure."
> —Marianne Williamson

The second part of this book is dedicated to helping you connect with your true self. But for now, just think of this process as the peeling of an onion, where the removal of each layer brings a new awareness and deeper understanding of the real you. The goal is to keep peeling away your "layers" until you reach the deepest possible understanding, thus creating a clearer reflection of your true self.

Fear

One of the biggest obstacles standing in your way is the real *f*-word: fear. Fear will immobilize you and shut you down. Fear is created by the mind in an effort to keep us safe. There's that word again: *safe*. Fear is the mind's mechanism for preventing our demise when it senses danger. If we aren't afraid of the sabre-toothed tiger, then we could just walk up and pat him on the back. We'd be lunch pretty

quickly, so fear is the mind's way of communicating when it predicts danger. Therefore, for most of us, our minds have decided that failure is dangerous business, naturally many fears will arise when we decide to take on something risky.

The good news is that you can learn to be free of fear. You can learn to acknowledge your fear instead of having it control you. You can feel the fear and do what you want despite the huge rush of adrenaline in your solar plexus. Nowhere in the definition of fear does it say "to stop." Recognizing that fear is just a tool created by the mind allows us to learn how to reprogram this conditioning such that it serves instead of hinders us. The key to being free of fear is to get out of our heads and back into our bodies in the present moment. When we are present to what is happening, we are no longer controlled by the stories in our minds. This presence gives us the ability to act *in spite of* our fear.

> *"You gain strength, courage and confidence by every experience in which you really stop to look fear in the face. You must do the thing which you think you cannot do."*
>
> —Eleanor Roosevelt

To say that I have a fear of heights is a gross understatement. Thousands of people who have been in my audiences have heard me describe in detail how I lose feeling in my legs when I get about 10 feet off the ground. The fear is very physical and

very real. However, I have devised a system of "making friends with fear," which I will share with you in a later chapter. "Being fearless" is about being free of our fear and learning to access our courage. Visit my website www.GinaML.com to see a short video of me being fearless as I plummet more than 500 feet towards the ground in an exhilarating bungee jump in New Zealand. This jump now acts as a metaphor for being fearless in all areas of my life. By the way, my legs still go weak when I hit the 10-foot-high mark

Feedback

Failure is the fast track to success because our failures clearly reflect exactly what stands between us and our true happiness. Failure is feedback, nothing more. Failure is just a reflection of something that isn't working on the inside. It doesn't hold any hidden meaning about our worthiness and doesn't mean that we shouldn't try. It is feedback about what worked and what didn't work. It contains all the necessary information for us to go back and change something on the inside so that we can produce a different outcome. If you can master the art of learning from your failures, you will find that you can literally direct your life exactly as you want it. We need to practice doing this. We need to unlearn our old habits and replace them with new, more empowering habits.

**FIRST, THERE ARE THREE CONCEPTS
TO REALLY UNDERSTAND:**

1. Happiness is a choice, not something caused by outside conditions.
2. NOT getting what you want is exactly what you need.
3. Failure is a good thing because it reflects back to you the exact thing that is standing in your way to getting what you want.

If you are like most people, at some point in your past you determined that in order to be happy you had to get something on the outside. Now you must realize that happiness is not something that is given to you by something on the outside. It's not a condition bestowed upon you by some other force. Circumstances don't make you happy or unhappy, but your choices do. Choice is a very powerful concept because it implies accountability and responsibility. We are all responsible for our lives, every single minute of them, regardless of what is happening to us. Think about it: In Benigni's *Life Is Beautiful,* how was it possible for Guido to remain happy while he was in a Nazi concentration camp? It was a conscious choice. The little boy didn't even realize what was happening the entire time because his father made a choice to retain control of his own happiness instead of abdicating it to his oppressors. This is a powerful *choice,* folks. Some of the happiest people

I have encountered are living with the worst of circumstances, and some of the unhappiest people I have ever
met live in a world of unlimited privilege. Happiness is
not circumstantial; it is a choice, plain and simple. Happiness isn't gotten, it's chosen.

Happiness is not a result of doing anything; it's a way
of being. For so long we have been brainwashed into
thinking that if we only had *something* then we could do
the things we want and would finally be happy. This is
called the "HAVE-DO-BE" paradigm. I had seen the concept
of HAVE-DO-BE in many books and seminars over the
years, but it wasn't until writing this book that I really
understood the significance of those three words. For
example, have you ever said, "If only I **had** more money,
then I could **do** what I really want and then I would finally
be happy"? The problem with this is that happiness is
always dependent upon first getting something. But if you
reverse this paradigm to "BE-DO-HAVE," then you can
first choose to be happy, which leads to doing things that
are consistent with this happiness and finally to having a
life that you love because you created it that way by being
happy. Venice Bloodworth had the paradigm figured out
way back in 1952 when she wrote, 'we must BE before we
can DO.'[1] Three whole chapters in this book are dedicated to
helping you create a new paradigm around BE-DO-HAVE.

Shifting from HAVE-DO-BE to BE-DO-HAVE is fundamental to intentionally creating an amazing life. You will

---

[1]Venice Bloodworth, *Key to Yourself* (Camarillo, CA: DeVorss & Company, 1952), 86.

find yourself suddenly free to choose happiness as your way of being and then allow it to direct the remainder of your life. That way, whether or not you get something becomes irrelevant to your happiness. You are finally free to be okay with NOT getting something. You are finally free to look at your failures as merely reflections. If you don't like what you see, then it is easy enough to change.

We have the power in each moment to be happy with the way life is, even if we aren't getting what we want. The two aren't related. If you are unhappy with the way your life is, then consider that you have created a meaning about the way things are that makes you unhappy. You have chosen to empower this self-created meaning, so therefore you have chosen to be unhappy. You are clinging to this meaning as if it were the absolute truth, and this is what is causing your unhappiness. But the meaning came from your past experiences and, in actuality, has nothing to do with your current situation.

> *"Men [and women] are disturbed not by the things that happen, but by their opinion of the things that happen."*
> —Epictetus

Perspective

Have you ever noticed how the same thing can happen to two different people with entirely different outcomes? For example, I once ran a marathon. This is not earth-shattering

for many people. But if you knew me, you would understand just how impossible it really was. I am not a marathon runner. In fact, at best I am a slow walker. But I run because I love to run—I love to feel the wind in my hair and the continuous meditative rhythm of my feet hitting the ground. On this particular day, I triumphantly crossed that finish line at a whopping 6 hours and 9 minutes. Now, most people who run are gasping, "Wow, why did it take you so long?" You can imagine how devastating it would be for a world-class runner to take that long to complete a marathon. I, however, was ecstatic, jubilant and even giddy for finishing the marathon in ONLY 6 hours and 9 minutes. You see, there was a particularly "dark" part of the race for me where I almost gave up. I didn't think I could finish. But in that darkest moment I learned what I was really made of. I learned to believe in myself for the first time in my adult life. I learned to choose happiness regardless of what was happening to me.

Finishing that race was one of the greatest things that ever happened to me because I finally learned to let go of my attachments. But, for others, it might have been devastating. It's all about the meaning that was attached to the result. For me, the meaning was powerful, so the result was powerful. It was a choice. A choice I made the moment I decided to finish that race, no matter what it took, no matter what it looked like. I chose to be happy well before I crossed the finish line, and it was the most invigorating experience of my life. I chose happiness FIRST. This was a change on the inside. As

soon as I changed on the inside, the outside immediately followed suit and the results reflected this change exactly.

Now, the next shift you need to make to be happy is to
the paradigm that *NOT getting what you want is exactly what
you need*. It doesn't matter what you get in life; your happiness doesn't depend on it. You get what you get and that's
the way it is. Everything that happens in your life is perfect
for you. It couldn't be any other way. Your life needs to
unfold exactly as it is unfolding because that's exactly what
you have chosen. Any failure is merely feedback about
what's happening on the inside. Failure contains all the
clues necessary for you to learn what is standing in your
way. Failure is actually a gift, a built-in mechanism that
contains all the answers that you are looking for.

How many times have you heard, "In hindsight, that
[devastating thing] was the greatest thing that ever happened to me"? For example, you really needed to leave for
work on time because you had a huge sales meeting, but
your children needed extra attention in the morning so
you were late for work. Because you were late leaving the
house, you missed being in a huge multi-car pileup on the
freeway. Has this ever happened to you? How many times
have you looked back on something with a new perspective and been happy that it turned out the way it did? This
occurs all the time.

Instead of relegating this experience to hindsight, I'd
like to suggest that you can trust in the wisdom of what is

happening *as it happens*. This will allow you to leverage the power of the experience such that you will be able to use it to your advantage immediately, instead of waiting for some vague time in the future when it will finally make sense. There are no accidents in the universe. Everything happens exactly as it should based on your choices every single day. It couldn't be any other way.

We attract what we think about and expect. Failure is an indication that something didn't work. There was a disconnect in the attraction process that led to an unwanted result. By understanding this concept, you can harness the lesson that exists in every single outcome you generate. Where did the disconnect occur? Was it in your choice about who you were being or was it in your actions? Were you consistent with your higher purpose? Were you being who you really are or were you trying to be someone else? Only you know for sure, and the only way to learn is to try. Later in the book you will see how understanding your personal vision is key

> *"I wanted a perfect ending. Now I've learned, the hard way, that some poems don't rhyme, and some stories don't have a clear beginning, middle and end. Life is about not knowing, having to change, taking the moment and making the best of it without knowing what's going to happen next."*
>
> —Gilda Radner

to identifying the opportunities in the results you generate. Remember, the first time you try to use failure will be the hardest, but if you persist, you can become a master at directing your life—simply by paying attention to the clues being reflected to you.

Failing is the greatest thing that can happen to you, *if* you learn to use it. If you learn to read it and act on it. The key to really leveraging failure is realizing that you have to change something on the inside in order for your outer-world results to change. If you don't, you are simply doing the same thing over and over again expecting different results. This will drive you crazy. To get something different, you have to try something different. The best way to decide what to do differently is to pay attention to your feedback—your failure—and then make a change on the inside. Hey, with this perspective, you just might find that failing is actually fun!

Another possibility is that you might begin to enjoy the process of living your life now, instead of waiting for something to happen "out there" before you love life. You might start to see that "going for it" is just as much fun, if not more than, "getting it." You might begin to notice the little nuggets of joy that exist everywhere in the present moment. As you become more aware of being happy in the present, you will finally be free to notice the little things in life that really matter. By shifting your focus from lack to abundance and gratitude, you allow yourself to expand, grow and live.

Joy

Joy comes from being alive and from being attentive to what is actually happening in the present moment, especially if we are pursuing what we want—going for it 100%. Then, trying to get what we want in life will no longer be such a burden. We'll be living life fully, and the results will be what they are. But so often we make our happiness dependent upon one moment of realizing a result instead of the thousands of potentially joyful moments spent preparing to achieve that result. We need to focus our efforts on being happy in those thousands of minutes and let the moment be what the moment is: a point of feedback, not a point of judgment. Then, once we get our feedback, we can adjust accordingly on the inside and try something new, something that will joyfully fill up the next thousand moments.

One thing that stands in the way of a blissful existence is the belief that we are somehow not worthy of it, that we don't deserve it. Perhaps we think that blissful existence is meant for someone else, but surely not for us because we have so many flaws or aren't smart enough or don't have enough money, and so on and so forth. NOT TRUE!

It is your birthright to live a joyful existence! It is your birthright to fully express your true self. It is your birthright to give your gifts to this world in all of their glory. Anything less is wrong. If you have been made to believe that you are not entitled to live your true life, then you have been lied to. We are all here to express our true purpose

and to leave our mark on the world in whatever way that is. We are all part of the same universe. We are all part of a divine creation, and it is our birthright to live out this existence in the most joyful way possible.

Life is a grand adventure that is meant to be experienced and lived. It is not meant to simply be survived, avoided or tolerated until you die. You are here to manifest the brilliance that exists deep inside you, regardless of what someone made you believe about yourself. It all comes down to choice, *your* choice about what you want it to be. There are many tools to help you experience the life of your dreams, but you must live consciously and with deliberate intent if you are to experience the full greatness of your being. You must learn to see the pictures that the Universe reflects back to you and use them to your advantage. You must start to see the beauty in all moments of your life and start living fully and passionately. If you keep waiting for someone to give you permission to live your true life, you might find yourself on your deathbed still waiting.

You need to remember who you really are and begin to reconnect with that true self. You need to honour your desires—those things that make your heart sing. You need to notice what gets your attention in life, because everything you need is laid out directly in front of you. You need to have courage and be brave when you begin to live the life of your dreams, because you will have many fears

that will attempt to thwart your efforts. You need to be able to look in a mirror and accept what you see. Acknowledging and understanding your fears is one of the greatest gifts you can give yourself. Being able to face your fear and "do it anyway" will allow you to move into a new relationship with what you believe is possible. This will create some space in which to manifest a new reality.

It all begins with the choices you make about who you are. You will find that your results reflect exactly how effective your choices have been. You can then choose to use your results to alter who you are being on the inside such that you produce different results on the outside. You can continue to master this cycle until you are able to direct your energy to produce exactly what you want. But it all starts with NOT getting what you want and learning to be grateful for that because it contains the biggest clues for how to live the life of your dreams. Again, your failures are the fast track to your success. They are no longer obstacles to be avoided, but rather your springboards to victory.

THREE SIMPLE STEPS WILL GIVE YOU ACCESS TO A LIFETIME OF JOY AND HAPPINESS

1. Choose a powerful way of being on the inside.
2. Do some things that are consistent with this choice in the pursuit of your goals.
3. Use your results as feedback to tweak your way of being.

It really is that simple. As humans, we love to create drama and complexity because that's how we were pro-grammed, but the reality is that life is really quite simple. The answers ARE right in front of you and you can be totally happy in this life—right now. This book is about shifting what you believe about failure and using it to access the power of the Universe. It is about being happy in the present moment, regardless of what is happening to you. It is about using what you see in the mirror to lead you closer to exactly what you want.

> *"You evolve not by seeking to go elsewhere but by paying attention to, and embracing, what's in front of you."*
>
> —Anonymous

*"Only those who dare to fail greatly
can ever achieve greatly."*

—Robert F. Kennedy

chapter 2

THE FEEDBACK LOOP OF LIFE

"I wasn't afraid to fail.
Something good always comes out of failure."
—Anne Baxter

This entire book is based on one premise: that failure is simply feedback. Failure is not what we have been led to believe. It is not a judgment that proves our inadequacy. It is not a reason to give up. It is not something to be ashamed of. It is not the Universe telling us, "It wasn't meant to be." Failure is feedback. Period.

At this point you might be asking yourself, "So what? What does that mean to me?" You see, if failure is feedback then you can use it as a tool to get exactly what you want. You can use "not getting what you want" to actually get what you want. You can start to look at life as a giant feedback loop. I know that some of you might be cringing at such a scientific-sounding notion. Your reaction might be leftover negative energy from a science course that got

the best of you. Not to worry. The feedback loop is actually quite easy to understand. A very simple definition is "a process that feeds back some of the output to the input of a system," and it looks something like this:

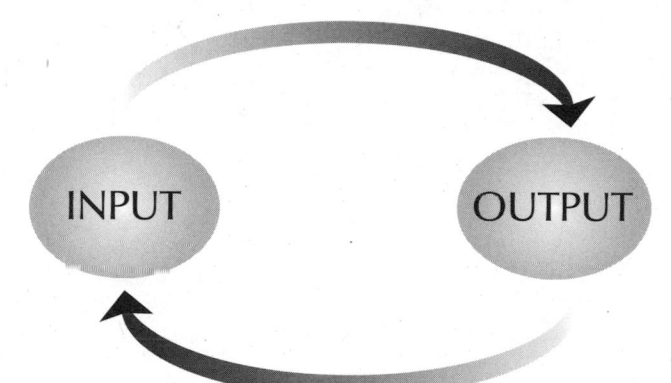

INPUT   OUTPUT

Basic Feedback Loop

As you can see, you can use the output to help manipulate the next input, thus achieving a more desired output next time around. Using this same logic, wouldn't it make sense that you could use your failures (output) to help you change (input) so that you can actually get what you want? Bingo!

Failure is a built-in answering system that actually points us in the direction of our dreams. Failure highlights the reality of what is showing up in our mirror of life. If we can learn to read and understand our failures, then we can get on the fast track to getting exactly what we want. The answers lie in the feedback—our failures. Say this three times to yourself: "Failure is feedback! Failure is feedback! Failure is feedback!" You are on your way!

A feedback loop always works in the same way, and you can use this understanding to help get what you want. You can use the information contained in your failures (output) to manipulate your next input so that your next output is closer to what you want. I call this process the "Feedback Loop of Life."

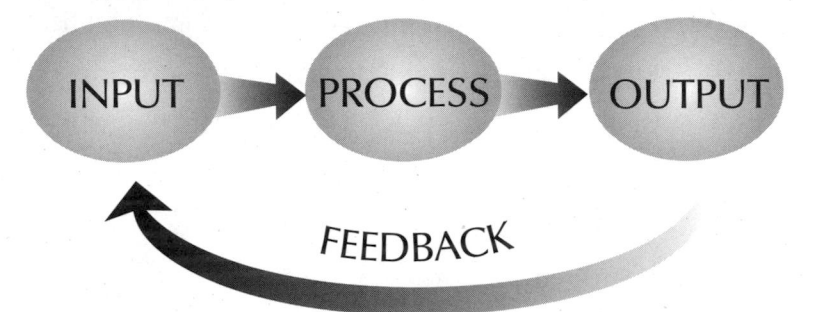

The Feedback Loop of Life

Life consists of a series of feedback loops. We want something (input), we do stuff (process) and we get an outcome (output). Sometimes we try to repeat the same loop over and over again, and other times we try only once. Basically, though, it's all feedback loops. Feedback loops all work the same way and are all governed by the same laws. Understanding how they work and the laws that govern them is the key to unlocking the secrets of getting what you want.

The classic example of a feedback loop is the thermostat. A thermostat has a desired set point for the temperature of the room. It is constantly monitoring the temperature. When the temperature falls below the set point, the thermostat

tells the furnace to turn on. The thermostat uses the feed-back to initiate a process to heat the room. When the temperature reaches the desired set point, the furnace uses the feedback again to tell the furnace to shut off.

Defining the Universe

Thanks to Einstein, we know that everything in the universe is energy in some form. His famous discovery of $E=mc^2$ changed the way all of life was understood. Any fragment of matter can be converted into an equivalent amount of energy. Likewise, all energy takes on a different form in the physical world. The universe is made up of both mass and energy and the two are interchangeable and convertible using Einstein's theory of relativity. In other words, mass is the visible part of the universe and energy is the invisible part. This applies to us as well. We are just a big bundle of energy. The human body is the physical part of this energy and our thoughts and emotions are the invisible part. Thoughts and feelings are more than just biochemical reactions; they are actually electromagnetic patterns of energy. We emit energy every day in the form of thoughts and emotions.

All energy in the universe is governed by Universal Laws. These are divine laws that cannot be broken or ignored. They simply are. Just as the law of gravity is in effect whether or not we know about it, so are the Universal Laws. Thanks to teachers such as Abraham-Hicks, we are now aware of

three major Universal Laws: the Law of Attraction, the Law of Deliberate Creation and the Law of Allowing. When we are in harmony with these laws, life flows effortlessly. Likewise, when we are not in harmony with them, life will seem to be a difficult struggle.

The Law of Attraction

Quantum theory suggests that the entire universe (including you and me) is energy vibrating at different levels. All energy vibrates at a unique fre-quency. When something vibrates at a unique frequency, it naturally res-onates with and attracts other things that have the same frequency. In other words, like attracts like. This is the Law of Attraction in a nutshell, and it applies to all energy in the universe. It is like two tuning forks; the vibration of one will subtly pro-voke vibration in the other until both vibrate together in harmony. And like a tuning fork, our thoughts and feelings emit specific energetic vibrations that externally resonate and attract frequencies that correspond to those vibrations.

> *"What you love you empower. And what you fear you empower. And what you empower you attract."*
> —Author Unknown

The Law of Attraction states that we get what we focus on. However, it is not enough to simply think about some-thing in order to get it. We also have to "feel" it because

our feelings are where the bulk of our energy gets transmitted into the universe and it is the energy that does the attracting. It is very important to be mindful of what we are thinking and especially feeling, because that is what we will get more of. When we have a thought that makes us feel good, we are aligned with attracting what we want. Likewise, if we have a thought that makes us feel bad, we are out of alignment with what we really want. If we focus on what we don't want, we will certainly get what we don't want. Our focus must be on what we want, not on what we are lacking. If we focus on lack, we will get more lack. The key is paying attention to how our thoughts make us feel and being mindful of staying with the thoughts that make us feel good.

Applying the Law of Attraction takes practice, but, remember, you have a built-in feedback mechanism—failure—that tells you how you are doing. If you don't get what you want, you will have received some feedback that tells you that you weren't clear about your attraction. In this case, you will either get what you want or you will get feedback you can use next time. Either way, you always *get* something. It makes me think of that "Got Milk?" advertising campaign. In this case, though, it would be "Got Feedback?" The clues contained in your failure can guide you to altering your attraction. Then you can try all over again to attract what you really want. Failure is just a measure of the outcome of your attempt

to attract something you want. You must use it to help master your ability to attract what you want.

Many of us have been conditioned to believe that we don't deserve to have the things we really want. I don't know why this phenomenon exists, but it seems that every single human being is ashamed to acknowledge her or his desires. At some point in life, somebody we trusted or loved told us that our desires were nonsense, unattainable and unrealistic. This is probably the single biggest reason people don't get what they want: They simply don't believe they deserve it. It doesn't matter how we came to believe this, but rather that we understand that this barrier exists. In order to fully benefit from the Law of Attraction, you have to be very clear about what it is you want, without any doubt or reservation. If you are unclear, you will have difficulty manifesting your dreams and thus will block the receiving of what you want.

A sure-fire way to know if you have any doubts or if you lack clarity is to observe your reality. If you feel resistance or if life feels "hard," there is likely a hidden doubt or lack of clarity underneath all your wanting. You need to address your doubt or lack of clarity before you can attract what you truly want.

I am here to tell you that it is your birthright to manifest a life of joy and happiness. Anything you might have been told to the contrary about what you want or what you should want is hogwash. Period.

Abundance

Contrary to popular belief, the universe is infinitely abundant. If everything is made of energy and energy is infinitely abundant, then it follows that everything is infinitely abundant. We find this wisdom in many ancient teachings and scriptures. Despite this knowledge, human beings have, sadly, created a culture of scarcity. And this causes us to attract more scarcity. Could it be that the global focus on scarcity is actually contributing to the alarming rise of poverty in the world? The key to attracting exactly what you want is to believe in the abundance of the universe. You must understand that if you focus on abundance, it is abundance you shall have.

> *"Cut not the wings of your dreams for they are the heartbeat and the freedom of your soul."*
>
> —Flavia

The Law of Deliberate Creation

To understand Universal Law #2 is to understand your own role in creating your reality. We have already established that Universal Law #1, the Law of Attraction, states that we get what we focus on. The Law of Deliberate Creation states that we can deliberately create anything we want, including the lives we want. We deliberately choose to attract the positive instead of the negative. We create our lives by choice. If we do not make this choice deliberately, we are simply creating randomly, by default, and

surrendering our powerful ability to attract that which we truly want. Most people don't understand that they can consciously create their life and they feel frustrated when life doesn't go their way. The key is being deliberate and clear about what we want and choosing to empower with emotions (energy) the thoughts that will attract it.

Consciously choosing to create what you want is a vital step in getting what you want. The best way to determine whether a thing is something you really want is to pay attention to your feelings. If the thought of having that thing in your life feels good, then you should go with it. Likewise, if it feels bad, you need to continue refining your desire until it feels good. Your feelings will clearly indicate whether you are focusing on what you really want or whether you are focusing on the lack of that thing. Feelings never lie.

Unfortunately, it is sometimes difficult to get in tune with our feelings. It takes practice. Most of us have been conditioned to live in our minds instead of our bodies. However, it is the body that houses the feelings. When we fall in love, we feel it in our bodies. When we see someone we love after a long trip, we feel a rush of emotion in our solar plexus. If you want to harness the power of deliberate creation, you must become mindful of what you are feeling. You must learn to be aware of when you are feeling good and when you are feeling bad. Feeling good leads to attracting the things you want, while feeling bad leads

to resistance and blockage to what you really want. Your feelings are your guide to whether your thoughts are focused on attracting what you want (feels good) or what you don't want (feels bad). It is futile to try to control your thoughts. They come and go without any real effort on your part. They are just there. The only thing you can really do is empower those thoughts that make you feel good and ignore the ones that don't. It's that simple. If it feels good, keep it; if it feels bad, let it pass by.

> "Ask and it will be given to you; seek and you will find; knock and the door will be opened to you."
> —Jesus Christ

The Law of Deliberate Creation goes hand-in-hand with the Law of Attraction. Once you understand that you can literally attract anything you want in life through the Law of Attraction, you can use the Law of Deliberate Creation to set about deliberately creating a life you will love.

The Law of Allowing

The final of the three Universal Laws is the Law of Allowing. This states that we must allow that which is happening to happen. If we are trying to attract something into our lives, we must allow it to come to us. Similarly, we must also allow that which is being attracted to others to go to them. If we are in congruence with the Law of Allowing, then we will experience no resistance in getting

what we want because we are allowing the Universe to flow. On the other hand, if we have any doubt or reservation about what we want, we will find ourselves in disharmony with this law and will experience resistance and hardship in getting what we want.

This is perhaps the most difficult law to fully embrace because it means allowing things to be exactly as they are, without judgment. It means allowing what we want to actually come to us. Remember, we get what we attract. If we focus on what we don't want or resist what is actually happening in any way, we will simply get more of the same. The Law of Allowing is really about looking in the mirror and understanding the accuracy of the reflection.

Carl Jung said, "What you resist persists." This is the Law of Allowing working in conjunction with the Law of Attraction. We must take our focus off the circumstance we do not want and turn it into something we do want, something that empowers us. Have you noticed that the "war against crime" has actually produced more crime? Instead, how about a focus on a "peaceful society"? This perspective is key for getting something different and a result that we want.

If we find ourselves getting more and more of an undesired result, that is a clue that we have some doubt about what we want. This feedback allows us to go back and change our energy so that we can actually attract what we want into our lives. We have to stop looking for what's wrong

and start looking for what's right. We must stop saying "no" to anything and start saying "yes" to the things we want. We have to stop making "war" on anything and start seeing "love" in everything. It is that simple. No joke!

When we allow the things we want to come into our lives, we are in a place of non-resistance, and those things can actually flow towards us. Our feelings are an indicator of whether we are in a state of allowing or a state of resistance. When we feel good, we can be sure we are in a state of allowing. Thus, in order to understand our level of allowing, we must pay attention to our feelings.

> *"Allow the world to live as it chooses, and allow yourself to live as you choose."*
> —Richard Bach

The Feedback Loop of Life

Ben Franklin said it first: "The definition of insanity is doing the same thing over again, expecting a different result." This is true when applying the Universal Laws. If we keep getting the same results, it means we have continued to do the same things. This is the Law of Attraction in action. We get what we attract. Period. If we aren't getting anything different, then we haven't changed what we are focussing on. Having the expectation that things will change on their own will drive us mad, because nothing will change that way.

To get a different output, we must change our input. This is where failure comes in mighty handy. Using failure

as feedback, we can actually change the input in our feed-back loop. Changing the input guarantees that we will get a different output. Insanity be damned!

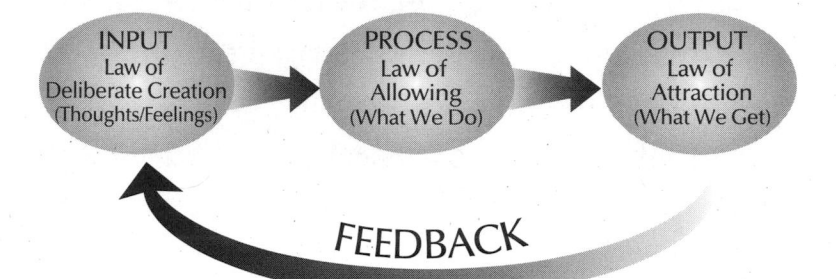

The Feedback Loop of Life

A basic feedback loop helps us use our output to change our input until we reach our desired result. In the case of the "Feedback Loop of Life," this means that we use our failures (output) to change our thoughts and feel-ings (input) such that we can actually achieve our desired result. It is that simple! Here's how it actually works:

- You decide on a clearly desired result. (**Deliberate Creation**)
- You generate the required vibrational energy to attract this result because you understand how the **Law of Attraction** works.
- You take inspired action along your path to the out-come, trusting that you are on the "right path." (**Law of Allowing**)
- At a point in time you will attract a certain result (output) according to the **Law of Attraction**.

- If it is your desired result, then you celebrate and move on to the next one.
- If it is not your desired result (i.e., you experience a failure), then you use the information to affect a change on the inside so that you can attract what you really want next time.

Recently my husband, Andrew, and I were experimenting with this process. Unbeknownst to me, Andrew was working on attracting $5,000 in extra money into his life that didn't come from any of our businesses. After a long day at work, I returned home to find a big envelope from the Canada Revenue Agency (CRA). My initial reaction was anxiety because I thought this could only mean an audit on our taxes. This extra work was not something I wanted in my life. In that moment, I made a conscious decision to trust the Universe on this one. I immediately shifted into the positive. Clearly, this was going to be a good thing. I just had to trust. I made a choice to shift my energy first.

When I finally opened the envelope, I learned that the CRA did, in fact, want to see all of our receipts from our big move across the country. As I was gathering the required receipts, I came across a worksheet provided by the CRA to ensure that I sent the right thing. It came to my attention that we had not submitted a large number of receipts because we didn't know that they were eligible. My accountant confirmed my discovery. We submitted the additional receipts along with the ones they were asking for. The end result

was an additional $6,500 in income tax returned to us. When I told Andrew about this windfall, he went pale. He said, "I had created the intention to attract an extra $5,000 into my life and had no idea how it was going to happen. I did not expect it to come from our taxes." Talk about the power of attraction!

This process repeats itself infinitely in life because we are always on a path to something. In some cases, we have been on the same path for years, and in other cases we tread along the path only once before reaching the desired result. The important thing to note is that this process doesn't end. We don't get to some elusive destination where they hand us a piña colada and say, "Congratulations! You have cracked the nut, so now you can just sit here." No, the process repeats itself over and over again for as many things as we desire. This makes me think of shampoo bottles that say, "Lather, rinse, REPEAT." That's life. Want it, go for it, REPEAT. Just like washing your hair.

BE-DO-HAVE

Another way to think about the Feedback Loop of Life is by understanding the BE-DO-HAVE concept, mentioned previously. As noted, most of us believe that we must HAVE something first before we can DO anything so that we can BE something. For example, how many times have you heard, "If I HAD more money I could DO what I really want and then I would finally BE happy"? This is backwards. How

do I know it's backwards? Because it is fundamentally impossible for the Universe to operate like this. It is energetically impossible. It simply cannot be. Check this out.

Based on the energetic laws of the Universe, energy attracts results, not the other way around. An energetic vibration is the FIRST thing that happens to put everything in life in motion. Where does the vibration start? With our thoughts. Put another way: Thoughts lead to Feelings, which lead to Actions, which lead to Results.

HAVE-DO-BE is impossible because that would mean that Results lead to Actions, which lead to Feelings, which lead to Thoughts. This contradicts the Law of Attraction. It is energetically impossible!

All we have to do to start having anything we want is reprogram the way we think. I hope you are as excited about this as I was when it hit me. The thing that makes me even more excited is that if we do not get what we want the first time (i.e., we have a failure), then we can use that feedback to correct our input right away. We know exactly what we do because the answer is sitting right in front of us. WOW!

Here is another representation of the Feedback Loop of Life using BE-DO-HAVE.

The Feedback Loop of Life

It indicates that if we do not HAVE what we want, then we use the information in our failure to manipulate our BEING (input) until we get our desired result. This is a critical distinction! Note that the accepted common belief is that if we do NOT get what we want, then we must go back and DO something different. This is flat out wrong and it will drive us crazy because doing something different doesn't necessarily change the outcome. The final outcome can only be affected by manipulating the input, which in this case is how we are BEING. To change what we have, we must change our thoughts and feelings or "energy."

I have two small children—the usual rambunctious and energetic kind. This has been known to stress me out at times. On one particular occasion, I was trying to get them to bed without much of a ruckus. It wasn't going

well. I kept thinking to myself, "If only they would behave better, I would be happy." Then it hit me. My being happy had nothing to do with them. I had chosen to empower my negative interpretation of the situation. I was living in the paradigm of HAVE-DO-BE. My feelings of insecurity as a parent dominated my thoughts. My physical world simply reflected that. Then, in that moment, I made a *different* choice. I chose to be happy with exactly what I had. I took the time to appreciate how amazing my children are and how good they are at reflecting my reality to me. I was thankful for who they were exactly as they were, rambunctious and all. It was like magic. The moment I let it go, the ruckus ceased. They instantly picked up on my new vibration and calmed down. I hadn't said one word. We finished our bedtime routine in peace and quiet.

Temporary Reality

Now, notice that I said the "final outcome" can only be affected by changing the input. This is another key distinction. Once we have a final outcome (i.e., the point in time where we either get what we want or NOT), then the only thing we can do to get a different result is change the input. However, there is a period of time between BE and HAVE, which I like to call "temporary reality." During this time, the energy has already been set in motion to attract the desired result. We have done our deliberate creating and attracting. We are now charged with the task of taking

"inspired" action towards the achievement of our goal. During "temporary reality," we are DOING a lot of things.

According to Universal Law, there is always a most straightforward path between BE and HAVE, between your "energetic reality" (input) and your "physical reality" (output). However, we must be fully congruent with the Law of Allowing in order to walk this most straightforward path. This is where most of us get tripped up—in the Law of Allowing. This is where most of the doubt resides, and hence this is usually where most desired results get missed. The Law of Allowing requires that we trust that what is put before us is perfectly aligned with our desired result and that the path we are on will lead us directly to it.

Much of the time our minds think they have a better idea. Much of the time our minds think they have "figured out" the most logical and safe way to get what we want. When the actual most straightforward path contradicts the mind's path, doubt arises and inspired action gets muddied with "logical action." It is important to remember that "doubt" is a feeling with a unique vibration and it sends a conflicting message into the Universe about what we are trying to attract. This vibration can override our original vibration, thus blocking the attraction of our desired result.

Remember the bonus income tax refund that my family received as a result of an audit. This was definitely not the "most logical" way to attract an extra $5,000, but it's how it happened for us.

Pay Attention to What Gets Your Attention

There is something you can do about this conflicting vibration such that it doesn't totally change your attraction and "rain on your parade." The Universe is always sending signs and signals as to which way is the most straightforward path to our desired result. The fact is that most of the time we miss the signals. You must "pay attention to what gets your attention" in order to know your right path. Whatever you notice in your life is what is trying to get your attention for a reason, based on what you said you wanted.

> *"Pay attention to what gets your attention."*
> —Gina Mollicone-Long

Nobody else notices what you notice. Nobody else cares about what you care about. This is because nobody else is trying to attract exactly what you are trying to attract for yourself. It is unique to you and therefore you must pay attention to what is happening to you, especially if you feel agitated by it. Agitation is usually a sign that your mind's safety zone has been breached. However, pushing through the other side of this agitation is where your most straightforward path can be found. You must pay attention to what gets your attention and then act on it in spite of any fear, doubt, mistrust or other unpleasant feeling that may arise. You have to trust in the laws of the Universe. They work. Always. Remember what Oprah said: "God first speaks to us in whispers...." This is what I am talking about. Paying attention to what

gets your attention will allow you to minimize the number of "cosmic two-by-fours" you get hit with.

Minor Feedback

As it pertains to the Feedback Loop of Life, inside the "temporary reality" there exists "minor feedback" from the Universe as to whether we are walking the most straightforward path. Paying attention to what gets your attention allows you to capitalize on this "minor feedback" so that you can correct your course to your desired result. The whole thing looks like this:

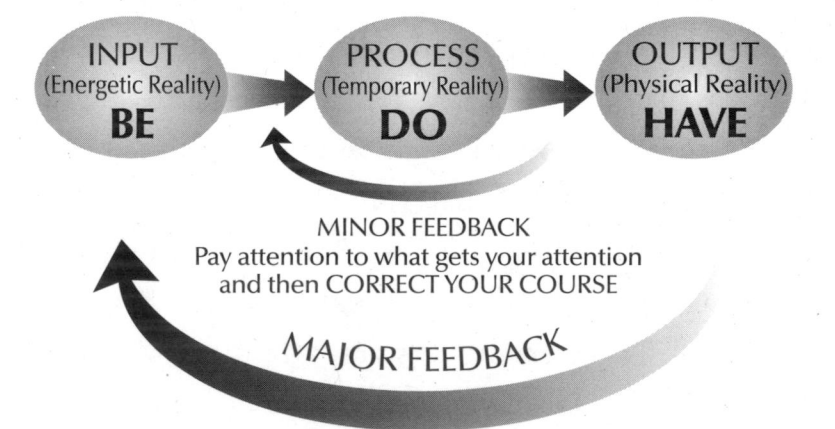

The key thing to remember in the Feedback Loop of Life is that we can always make course corrections using minor feedback from the Universe. This means that up until we have the "physical reality" or "final outcome," we can actually change what we are doing and alter our output. These course corrections are the only time that changing what we DO

instead of who we are BEING will alter the outcome. During "temporary reality," there is a lag between our initial desire (energetic reality) and the physical manifestation (physical reality). There is always a most straightforward path, but we don't always take it. When we stray from this most straightforward path, the Universe sends us signals. If we notice them, we are able to change our actions, thus altering our course to the final outcome.

Let's take the example of finding the perfect job. You generate the intention to attract the perfect job and then really feel the energy. During your "temporary reality," the Universe sends you signals to guide you directly to your dream career. You either heed these signals or ignore them based on your mind's plan. You notice that you always seem to stumble upon information relating to animals and their well-being. You direct all your charitable funds towards the welfare of animals, you attend rallies and fundraising galas, you volunteer at the animal shelter and you love having pets. These encounters get your attention because you notice that a lot of your spare time is spent on caring for animals. Your mind decided early on that while animals were a worthy charity, they weren't a powerful career choice. Your mind decided early on that a powerful career choice was in marketing. However, if you pay attention to what gets your attention, you just might find otherwise. If you were to decide to trust in the process, you just might

discover that a career involving animals is exactly what you have been looking for all these years.

You can alter your course during the "temporary reality" until the point in time when you either get what you want or NOT. Once you have a definitive "yes" or "no" as to whether you got what you wanted, you MUST adjust the input (BE) in order to generate your desired result (HAVE). It is not enough at this point to simply go back to actions (DO) because you will have missed the critical stage involving the Law of Attraction and generating the appropriate energy to attract your desired result.

The key to really using the Feedback Loop of Life is understanding when it is okay to adjust our actions and when we must adjust our energy to get what we want. Here is the secret: If you haven't yet had your final result, then there is still time to change what you are doing in order to stay on your path. Once you definitely have a final result, if you did NOT get what you want then you MUST go back and change how you are BEING because it is your input that needs adjusting.

For example, if you had decided not to heed the signals from the Universe and you continued to ignore your "animal instinct," you would never try working in that field. Instead, your mind's plan includes getting a high-powered job at a multi-national corporation with all the right brands. You are good at what you do and you enjoy the power that

comes with your job. After a while you find that you are again working ridiculous hours and you never take a vacation and you just worked on a brand that fundamentally violates your personal values. Busted again! At this point, you must go back and redo the whole process starting at the input. You must go back and change your energy around attracting the perfect job. You might have to clear some old patterns in order to do this. I'll cover that in more detail later in the book. Once you have a final result, you can only use the feedback to go back to the input and change it.

NOT getting what we want (aka "failure") is a gift because it contains all the information we need to adjust our input energy (BE). Once we begin to disengage from

> "I have not failed. I've found 10,000 ways that didn't work."
>
> —Thomas A. Edison

the judgments we have about our failures, then we become free to utilize them to our advantage. Once we master the art of learning from our failures, we become masters of attracting anything we want.

chapter 3

BE – THE ENERGETIC REALITY

*"Often people attempt to live their lives backwards:
they try to have more things, or more money, in order to
do more of what they want so they will be happier. The
way it actually works is the reverse. You must first be
who you really are, then, do what you need to do, in
order to have what you want."*

—Margaret Young

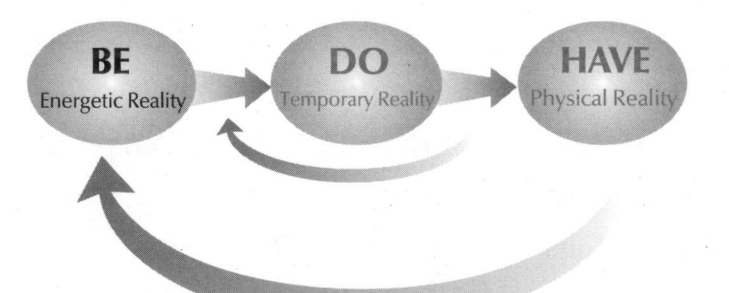

Being who we are is the most important, most difficult and most often overlooked part of the entire process of attracting what we want. As discussed, who we are being sets the stage for what we attract. If we are

not conscious about who we are being, then it is anyone's guess as to what we will get. Remember that we are human beings, not "human doings" and, as such, everything we experience is a result of who we are being—not the other way around. There is no such thing as one "true reality," only our interpretation of what we are experiencing, which is a direct result of who we are being. It is a direct result of the energy we have decided to empower in that moment. When we empower high-vibrational (positive) energy, we tend to only experience the positive things in life. Likewise, when we empower low-vibrational (negative) energy, we tend to only experience life's negative aspects.

> "We don't see things as they are. We see them as we are."
>
> —Anaïs Nin

Being is one of those words that gets overused and therefore its meaning becomes somewhat ambiguous. I'll be the first to admit that I had difficulty understanding this part—the part about "being." I thought I understood, but I never saw the whole picture—until I started learning about the Law of Attraction and how things are attracted to like energy. Then it clicked. "Being" is an energetic state, not a "doing" state. I realized that in order to attract effectively we must be mindful of the energy we are putting out by who we are being. "Being" is all about our energy.

As I overheard a conversation the other day, the concept of "being" totally clicked for me. One man was trying

to explain BE-DO-HAVE to the others in his group and he said something like, "If you want to BE a millionaire and HAVE a million dollars, then you have to DO what it takes to get from A to B." This did not sit right with me, but I couldn't put my finger on why until later when I became clear that what he said wasn't the way I understood BE-DO-HAVE with respect to the Law of Attraction.

What I realized was that in order to attract that million dollars, a person first had to "BE a millionaire." I know it sounds the same, but it is not. We have to "BE a millionaire" ENERGETICALLY so that we can literally attract the million dollars. If we are being a millionaire, then "the picture of a millionaire" would not be complete without a million dollars in our hands. The Universe abhors a vacuum, so when it sees someone "being a millionaire" (energetically) without the million dollars in her hands, it goes, "Ahhh, she is being a millionaire but doesn't have the physical million dollars. We'd better get it into her hands pronto so we can complete the whole picture." Being a millionaire is not something we become but rather it is an energy we assume FIRST before we ever get the million.

You see, if we assume the "being" energy in the present tense, we have essentially created a vacuum because there is a gap between our energy and our physical surroundings. The Universe goes into hyper-overdrive to fill this gap such that our physical surroundings match our energetic vibration. Remember that, based on the Law of Attraction,

our energetic vibration determines what we attract in life. This means we have to assume the vibration of what we want BEFORE we can physically have it. Then, based on Universal Law, it has no choice but to appear in our physical surroundings in order to match our vibration.

This might feel woo-woo weird for you and it may be the first time you've heard it, but I am telling you that this is the key to really using the Law of Attraction in a powerful way. You must assume the "BEING" energy IN THE PRESENT TENSE. You must assume the "BEING" energy of what you want as if you WERE ENJOYING IT RIGHT NOW! The reason you have to do this as if it were "right now" is that if you really did have it "right-now" you would be feeling pretty good. It is these good feelings that are the key to launching the Law of Attraction. I understand that your mind is likely telling you something like, "But I am NOT enjoying it in the present tense, so this whole exercise is nonsense and I feel stupid." Please remember that this is just your mind talking and it doesn't necessarily like this whole process because it is outside its comfort zone. Give your mind a mental hug—it really needs it.

I know this can be hard to digest. Believe me, I have spent countless hours trying to wrap my own head

> "It is important from time to time to slow down, to go away by yourself, and simply Be."
> —Eileen Caddy

around it. This is a great time to engage all five senses, so grab a pencil for this next exercise.

SENSE-ITIZE YOUR DESIRE

Let's say that you want to have a million dollars. This is your desired result: one million dollars. First, you have to BE a millionaire. So, let's get into your pretend "time machine" and go to the point in time where you ARE a millionaire. What does it feel like? Describe it in as much detail as you can and make sure you focus on what that feels like:

- What do you see in your "millionaire reality"? How do those things make you feel? It could be fancy clothes, a shiny car, a new house. Really describe it in as much detail as you can and be sure to identify how you feel in this place. Is it happy? Excited?

- What do you hear in your "millionaire reality"? How do those things make you feel? It could be classical music in your box at the opera or the sound of the ocean at your beach house or the sound of your golf club hitting the ball. Get into the sounds and try to identify how you feel during it all.

- What do you smell in your "millionaire reality"? How do those things make you feel? This could be the smell of bread baking in your new kitchen or the new-car smell of your dream automobile. What feelings do you have when you smell these things?

- What do you taste in your "millionaire reality"? How do those things make you feel? It could be beluga caviar or a fine bottle of wine. What feelings do these tastes evoke in you?

- What do you touch in your "millionaire reality"? How do those things make you feel? It could be the coolness of your new leather furniture or the coarseness of the sand between your toes on your holiday or perhaps the rush of wind in your hair while you drive your new convertible. How do these things make you feel?

Once you have really captured the energy of "BEING" a millionaire, you must embody that energy. Make it a part of you. You do this by relating your feelings to your thoughts. Then, take this "millionaire energy" and get back in your time machine and come back to the present. You have the "BEING a millionaire" energy with you and you can take it with you wherever you go. Then, several times a day, get into that "feeling" place of "being a millionaire." When you do, the Law of Attraction is in full motion and it will only be a matter of time before your physical reality matches your energetic reality. The things you do during this temporary reality are not as important as maintaining a strong vibrational match to what you want. You would be better to focus your efforts on sustaining the positive energy in order to speed up the process of attraction.

Choice

Nothing in life happens to us by accident. Everything is a result of the choices we have made. Everything is a result of what we have attracted based on our choices. *Everything.* No exceptions! Furthermore, we are ultimately responsible for the consequences of our choices. Who we are BEING is a choice we make whether we are aware of it or not. We either choose this BEING deliberately or we choose it by default. Either way, it is our choice and nobody else can choose it for us. Even when we do nothing, we have made a powerful choice.

Some people get upset when I say this because a lot of bad things happen in this world and many times these bad things happen to good people. How can this be? First of all, when something bad happens, it doesn't mean that WE are bad; it just means that somehow we have attracted something at that "bad frequency." I don't know why it happens, but it definitely does. Please remember, attracting something "bad" or "undesirable" does NOT mean that we are bad. It simply means that on a vibrational level, what we have gotten is what we are attracting. Second, even when bad things are happening, we still have a choice. Circumstances do not dictate our state of mind; we do. We literally have the power to choose how we feel in each and every moment of life.

In the second part of this book, we will explore how practicing forgiveness and gratitude are two of the most

influential choices we have in regaining our power to be happy. We can choose to be happy regardless of the circumstances, if we are willing to heal the wounds that present themselves in the reflection of this mirror we call life.

Accountability

We are accountable for what we experience in life. As noted, our choices dictate our experiences. This distinction is important because many of us have the tendency of blaming others, the situation or even happenstance for our own circumstances. Blaming incorrectly shifts the accountability from ourselves to forces "beyond our control" that we believe are conspiring against us. Based on the Law of Attraction, this is energetically impossible. We get what we attract and we attract things that match our vibrational frequency. Therefore, we are ultimately responsible for what we have attracted in life. And we have attracted these things based on who we have chosen to BE.

The definition of accountability is "responsibility to someone or for some activity." The definition of responsible is "being the agent or cause." When we are accountable for our choices, we are acknowledging the role we play in directing our choices and their subsequent consequences. Being accountable for your choices is a very important step in being able to choose powerfully.

A few years ago I had the opportunity to train with a guru from India. He was an incredible and enlightened

human being. Just being in his presence was an energetic thrill. I could literally "feel" his positive and powerful vibrations. It was almost impossible NOT to be happy and positive in his presence. He spoke of how responsibility is our "ability" to "respond" to our choices in life. The greater our ability to respond to our choices, the more power we have to craft our experience (and our impact on others around us). Sharpening this "ability to respond" is key to maximizing our potential.

Being Happy

Happiness, in and of itself, is a choice. It is not the result of anything other than a choice. Either we choose happiness or we choose otherwise, and we can make this choice at any time. Things don't make people happy. Circumstances don't make people happy. Only our choice to be happy can make us truly happy. Happiness is an energy, a vibration. Remember that all vibrations have their genesis in what we choose to think and feel. This is BE-DO-HAVE. We don't get happiness from doing something. First we choose happiness, and then we do things from a place of happiness.

Notice whether you are having trouble agreeing with this concept of choice. If so, you have probably relinquished your power to be happy. You may believe that someone or something else holds the key to your happiness. You likely believe that you need to have some elusive

"thing" before you can really be happy. I am here to tell you that this is simply not true. Your ability to be happy whenever you want is inside you right now. The only thing you need to do to be happy is to CHOOSE to be happy. Happiness is a way of being.

At any time, you can get into your "time machine" and travel to your "happiness reality." How does it feel? Describe it in as much detail as you can. The more often you visit this place, the more often you will truly feel happiness in your life. Then you will finally start to attract those things into your life that support this "happy energy." Then guess what you will have more and more of? You got it—happiness!

Although you can choose happiness at any time, there will still be times when you feel particularly unhappy.

> "I have learned silence from the talkative, tolerance from the intolerant and kindness from the unkind. I should not be ungrateful to those teachers."
>
> —Kahlil Gibran

These times provide you with the clarity to define what it is you DO want. It is possible, in fact, to be okay or even content while going through a difficult period. We have been conditioned to avoid unhappiness. We have not been taught to view these difficult periods as necessary requirements for growth. We have not been taught to trust these times. Through the experience of that which causes us unhappiness,

we will likely have a revelation about what is standing in our way to happiness. Remember, it is in times of greatest distress that we discover the clarity about what we want. It is by experiencing the deepest dark that we come to appreciate the light. Our world is defined by duality. Getting what we do NOT want is sometimes the key to really understanding what we do want.

I remember being in one of my first careers at a prestigious multi-national company. It was very corporate and sensible. My parents and grandparents loved it because it was secure. I, on the other hand, was miserable. There were days when I would cry in the shower before going to work because I really didn't like my job. I knew deep in my heart that it was not my calling. Then one day it hit me. I started writing down all the things I disliked about my job. I had a list of what I did NOT want. Then I just flipped it right on its head. I wrote down the exact opposite of every single thing on that page. In that moment my first company, Goddess Concepts, was born. Instantly, I could finally appreciate that my life had to get really bad before I would finally stick my flag in the ground and stand up for what I wanted. It took sheer misery to lead me to make a different choice.

> *"Everything has its wonders, even darkness and silence, and I learn, whatever state I may be in, therein to be content."*
> —Helen Keller

Being Passionate

The state of passion is another powerful form of BEING. When we are BEING passionate, we are acting from our true selves. We are responding to the innate drive within us to pursue what we love. To be passionate about something means we are able to throw ourselves completely into something without regard for anything but the present moment. When we are being passionate, we are in a heightened state of emotion, which is the best way to attract what we want. It is important to note that the definition of passionate is "capable of, having or dominated by powerful emotions." If we connect this with the fact that the Law of Attraction is governed by energy produced by "feeling" something, we are more likely to attract what we want when we are BEING passionate about getting it. The more we act from our passion, the more congruent we are being with our true selves.

What are you passionate about? Can you identify the things you absolutely love to do? One way to do this is to recall a period in your life when time seemed to stand still or you totally lost track of time. Some people call this "being in the zone." I know that there have been times when I have been writing or creating a new product and I look up and eight hours have passed, though it only felt like five minutes. I have become accustomed to noticing when the things I am doing are driven by my real passions versus when I am acting out of obligation or conditioning.

I mean, let's face it, do you ever feel like you are in "the zone" when you are doing something you do not love to do? This is a clue that perhaps your passions lie elsewhere. By paying attention to what gets YOUR attention, you should be able to hone in on the things you are truly passionate about. I can guarantee that this list will be different for every person on this planet. Each and every one of us has come to this earth to make a unique contribution, and it is each of our responsibility to identify that unique contribution and to express it to its fullest.

PASSION REKINDLING

- Grab a piece of paper and give yourself exactly two minutes on the clock.
- Brainstorm, without editing, all the things you love to do.
- If you find it too difficult to name the things you love to do, then start out by first listing the things you do NOT love to do. Usually listing what you do NOT love to do helps you see the things you do love to do.
- Then take another two minutes to brainstorm, without editing, a list of people you absolutely love to be around. People who energize you.
- Now merge these lists with the intention of ranking your passions.
- Look for patterns and similarities between what you like to do and who you like to be around. You will be astonished to see that answers are right in front of you.

My mission in life is to reflect the light that is in each and every one of us. My commitment is to show up for people and reflect back to them their greatness, ingenuity and unique abilities. This is what gets me out of bed in the morning. I experience a special joy and peacefulness when I am congruent to this mission. When I show up for people I get to witness their greatness, and this is the only way I can truly experience my own. I can only get what I need when I give it to others. This is a really important point: I get what I truly want when I *give it away* to others!

> *"Let the beauty of what you love be what you do."*
> —Rumi

My biggest challenge is to choose to reflect the light that is in each of us. There are times when I don't want to experience my own light. In these times, I make a poor choice to reflect the lower-vibration, dark qualities in others. No one wins as a result of this choice. This is my life work—to refuse to give in to my programming that tells me something is wrong. Someone once said to me that I needed to have the discipline to shine forth with love in all situations. Each day I wake up with the intention to do just that.

Being Fearless

The dictionary definition of fearless is "free from fear." It is important to note that nowhere in this definition does it imply "without fear." Being fearless is not about eliminating

fear; it is an actual state of freedom from fear itself. We do not have to get rid of our fear in order to act powerfully, but we do need to develop the capacity to be free from fear. We can accomplish this by acknowledging and honouring our fear. We must remember that fear is the mind's way of protecting us from danger. Fear is a signal from the mind that we should not continue doing what we are doing because there is a perception of danger in our activity. However, our minds don't realize that the fear was probably created in childhood and may no longer serve us in the present. The only way to override our innate fear is to understand what we are afraid of and then act in spite of the fear.

If you take a moment to identify the root cause of your fear, you will likely be able to find some freedom from it. This process is helped by not only understanding your fear, but actually being grateful for having it. By "thanking" your fear, you are acknowledging that it has served you in the past. The important thing is that you recognize that it doesn't serve you in the present. If you work out the issues underneath your fear, you will find immense freedom.

I mentioned earlier that one of my biggest fears is the fear of heights. Even though I have spent countless hours working on myself to understand the root cause of this fear, I still feel its impact. Does this mean that I let it control me? Absolutely not!

Numerous events in my life have required me to act in spite of the fear that was running through my body. The

most successful of these endeavours has always occurred when I was in a state of gratitude and acknowledgement towards my fears. The ability to be afraid and still do the things that scare me has always been the strongest when I was in tune with my fear and not trying to subdue or suppress it. This doesn't mean that the fear goes away—far from it. In fact, today when I am up high I still feel as scared as I did before I even identified it as an opportunity. The only thing that has changed is who I choose to be in the presence of my fear—I am "fearless" and this shifts everything.

One observation I have made about great people is that they always exhibit two key qualities: passion and fearlessness. I find it fascinating to think about great people as "normal" people with fears and worries similar to mine. As human beings, these emotions are inescapable and yet many people in the course of history have managed to do great things in spite of feeling fear, doubt and worry. I believe that the difference is that great people are able to master their "being" in a way that attracts the things they see possible. Most great people are driven by a clear vision of what they stand for. This vision is congruent with their true self and hence they are able to be passionate about what they believe in. Their cause is so motivating to them that this passion enables them to also be fearless in the pursuit of what they want. Undoubtedly, they feel fear many times throughout the course of their lives, but the combination of passion and clarity allows them to act in spite of their fear

in order to achieve great things. Being passionate and fearless are two powerful ways of being that give us access to the same greatness achieved by prominent people throughout history. It always starts with how we are being.

FEAR FEEDBACK

Take a moment to get in tune with your fears. Fear is just another form of feedback in your life. Fear is the way to communicate that you do not feel safe. The real need being expressed is to feel safe and secure. The real way to do this is to go inside yourself and determine what you need in terms of comfort and love. By changing the way you take care of yourself when you are afraid, you will find that your fears no longer run your life. The following exercise will help you to see which of your fears holds the most feedback for you.

- Make a list of all the fears that come to mind. (Don't edit this list, just brainstorm.)
- Now, rank your fears from highest to lowest such that your biggest fear is at the top of the list.
- Pick one of the "Top 5" fears on your list to use for the rest of this exercise.
- Close your eyes and try to get into the feeling of your fear. How does your body feel when you are really experiencing this fear? Try to stay present.
- Can you remember where you developed this fear?
- Think about what this fear has cost you in your life. What joy have you missed?

- Imagine what you could do to help comfort your-self when you are afraid. How can you take care of yourself?

- What actions would you take if someone you loved was experiencing this fear? Would you hug them, talk softly, whisper encouraging words? Whatever you would do for them, you must do for yourself.

Your Greatness

As I mentioned earlier in this chapter, it is my belief that every human being brings a unique potential to this earth, something only she or he can cultivate and carry to fruition. This unique gift cannot be duplicated by anyone else. The deliverance of this gift is wholly dependent on the individual to realize. It is also my belief that every person has a responsibility to this world to understand, develop and manifest her or his unique gift to the absolute limit of her or his abilities.

It's time that you stop playing small in this world, hoping to get by unnoticed. You were put on this earth to bring out your fullest potential and make your unique contribution in the biggest way possible. You are entitled to a life complete with unconditional love and unlimited joy. It is there for you to take, if you want it. It all begins with who or what you are "being." This begins with a choice, a decision made by you about how you will conduct

yourself in this world. The consequences of this choice are also your responsibility because the Universe can only act according to what you set in motion. Your physical reality is simply the result of matching your physical environment with who you are already being in your energetic environment. The key to the entire process begins with and rests upon your "being."

Remember, paying attention to what gets your attention is one of the most powerful tools you have. If you notice something, then it must be important to you; therefore, the things you notice are "clues" as to what your unique contribution is to be. What is it going to take for you to realize what is at stake in this world? What "thing" is going to push you out of your comfort zone such that you choose to live to your fullest potential? What is it going to take for you to see the importance of changing who you are "being" such that you can finally begin to create a different story with a different ending, one that is filled with joy, happiness and love?

> *"Be the change that you want to see in the world."*
> —Mahatma Gandhi

It would be wise to focus on understanding how to master the art of "being," because therein lies the power to attract absolutely anything you want in life. You must create consciously and then maintain the energetic vibration for as long as possible. In other words, you want to

raise your vibration such that you can attract whatever it is you want, and then you must focus on maintaining this high-vibrational state for as long as possible. The more accomplished you become at maintaining a powerful way of being for a long time, the more successful you will be at attracting exactly what you want. Later in this book I will cover specific things you can do as well as things to avoid in order to master this step. You can also download a free report on raising and maintaining your energy levels from my website www.GinaML.com.

"Being" is the master input variable in the "Feedback Loop of Life." It is the most important variable we can manipulate in order to achieve our desired output. If we are faced with the disappointing reality of NOT getting what we want, we can finally use this to our advantage. We can begin to view our failures as the gifts that they are because they contain the very information about what is standing in our way. If we adjust our way of being based on what our failure is trying to show us, we will be well on our way to attracting exactly what we want in life. The key to using our failures is understanding how we can change who we are BEING versus trying to go back and DO things over and over again. The energy with which we attract things in life is tied completely to the energy we emit with our thoughts and feelings when we decided to BE a certain way. We must learn to master our thoughts and feelings such that they are congruent to what we want to attract. We

must learn to BE our result long before we hold it in our hands. Then it's just a matter of time before the Universe aligns our physical reality with our energetic reality.

It is no secret that our world is in desperate need of powerful individual contributions. We are in a tumultuous time of change, a time fraught with discord and distress. There is a silver lining, however, in all of this uncertainty. The contrast provided by the current circumstances gives us a rich and colourful canvas from which to create a new reality. The

> *"When you take a stand, other people find out who they are."*
> —Werner Earhart

depth of despair offers with it new heights of joy. The observation of what is currently transpiring on this planet allows us to create a new and vibrant vision for our world. Perhaps a desperate and despondent worldview is what is needed as the catalyst to inspire us to stand up for what we really believe in. Perhaps this is what we need in order to be able to identify what really matters to us. Perhaps this is needed to remind us why we are here and of the unique contributions we, and only we, can make.

What Is Your Finish Line?

This is the part of the book where you get to focus on exactly what you want, where you get to create your personal vision. This vision will be the foundation for every action you take. It will be the reason you get out of bed

in the morning, especially when you feel like sleeping in. This is where you take a stand for what you believe in, for what is important to you. This is where the real you finally shows up.

You might be confused by the term *vision* because everyone out there has a different definition of the word. Mine is simple: A vision is literally something you *see*.

LOOK AROUND

- Close your eyes and start to create your personal vision.

- What do you see for yourself?

- Look around. Describe the situation. The more detail you can describe (in the present tense, please), the more vivid your vision will become.

- Use all five senses: What do you see, hear, taste, smell and touch?

- Use your other senses, your sixth sense, your "spidey sense." What does it feel like in your vision? How does your body feel in your vision?

- What do you see as possible for this world? What matters to you?

Now, let's create your finish line. You need a succinct way to describe your personal vision such that it rolls off your tongue in 30 seconds or less. You will be able to use this vision as your "working example" in the following

chapters, so spend the time now to get it right for you. One thing I tell my workshop participants and clients when I lead this exercise is that there has to be a definitive way to measure the success or failure of your vision. It has to be clear and measurable; otherwise, you will not receive any useful feedback when you get your results. There needs to be a point in time where you can confirm whether you have achieved your goal or not. If you don't get what you want, then you will have gained the vital feedback that will help you adjust your energy appropriately so that you can try again.

At this time I also need to mention limits. Your vision should push right past the edge of your limits. You need to strive for a vision that you cannot even hope to achieve in this lifetime. What?!? The reason for this is twofold: first, if you have no expectation of achieving this personal vision, then you will not be disappointed at each attempt and you will really be open to the feedback that you get from the Universe. Second, when your vision is huge, it can inspire and include others with similar visions. Collectively, you will engage in a "mega-vision," and the power of the group vision will be more potent than the individual visions. The greatest leaders of the world have huge visions that enroll others and take years and years to come to fruition. Think of Martin Luther King Jr. or Mother Teresa. Their visions were not small. You need to think big!

Guiding Values and Principles

It is all well and good to know what your finish line is when you have the luxury of thinking about your life as a series of isolated events. But in actuality life is dynamic and always changing. True, everything always works out according to the Universal Laws, but the reality is that there are 6 billion people on this planet, all sending energetic signals at the same time, so there is bound to be some congestion as everything gets sorted out to perfection. It is very helpful to know what it is that guides you so that as life happens to you at breakneck speed you can act accordingly. Values are a set of statements that help guide your direction when you arrive at a crossroads.

Take a moment to consider what you value. For example, I really value kindness. It is very important to me to be kind to others and for others to be kind to each other and to me. A guiding value is something you feel strongly about and are willing to take a stand on.

CHOOSE YOUR BATTLES

It's important to "choose your battles," as they say. Usually our "battles" are over those things in life that we value a great deal. Now let's take an inventory of your values.

- List all the things in your life that are very important to you and that you "value." Don't edit this list.

- Rank your values from most important to least important.
- Combine similar values or reword your list such that you end up with about 10 powerful, guiding values.

Another tool you may find useful is to define your principles. Principles are more specific than values because they encompass detailed instructions on how you will live your life (how you will BE). They usually include multiple values along with guiding actions in specific circumstances. For example, in one of my companies, www.criticalpathfinders.com, we have a corporate identity statement that includes the following principles (obviously there are many more):

- Our work is fun!
- We are dedicated to making this world a better place!
- We focus on the solution, not on the problem!

"Nature never repeats herself, and the possibilities of one human soul will never be found in another."

—Elizabeth Cady Stanton

YOUR PERSONAL GUIDE

Use the values you listed above to create some guiding principles for your life. The end goal is to have a set of statements that will help you make decisions, especially when you are under pressure.

- Make a list of situations where your values might be tested.

- Match up the situations with your values.

- Derive a description of what you would like to see in those situations based on what is important to you.

- Combine and rework these statements until you have 5-10 guiding principles.

- Print these out and place them where you can see them to remind yourself of what is important to you.

chapter 4

DO – THE TEMPORARY REALITY

"Do…or do not. There is no try."
—Jedi Master Yoda, from *The Empire Strikes Back*

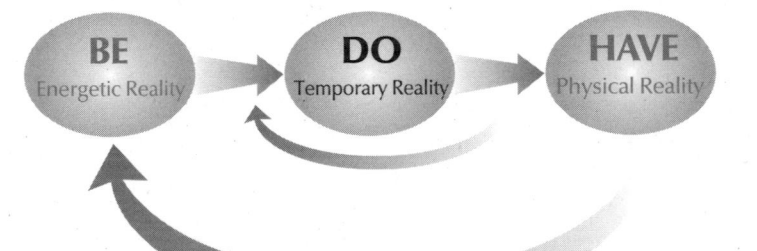

This next discussion is about the part of life the majority of us feel most comfortable with—the "doing" part. It is the most tangible part of our physical existence and, often, therefore, it is perceived as the *only* part of our existence. When we are focused on "doing" things, the spiritual or energetic component of our existence is usually forgotten. Many people mistakenly believe that simply changing what they do will really affect their outcomes.

That being said, doing is a very important part of living in the real world. What really matters is how inspired our actions are. Are they coming from your true self and inspired by your "energetic reality"? Are they trying to serve your ego and its version of what you want? Are they based in fear or abundance?

If you look at the diagram on the previous page, you can see that "doing" is part of the "temporary reality" that exists between your energetic reality and your physical reality. Once we set in motion a new energetic reality by focusing our energy and changing how we are BEING, we will experience a lag in time before we physically see the manifestation of our dreams in the "real world." During this temporary reality, we will need to DO things. What's important is to focus on doing things that are aligned with our energetic reality and consistent with who we want to BE.

The other main distinction about "doing" is that this is the part of life where we can check in on our energy to determine if we are indeed on the path we want to be on. It's like going from A to B on a map. Potentially, there exist many different routes to get from A to B. The important part is to stay on course so that we arrive at point B. What is really important is knowing that there is a most straightforward path from A to B and that if we pay attention and trust in the process, we will find this path. Some people call this "faith," and I can't think of a better definition. Having faith means knowing "It's all good" even when it might appear otherwise.

The actions that fill your day are all part of the fulfillment of your dreams, and if you pay attention to the details, you will find yourself approaching life with ease. A wise person once said to me, "If you have a choice between the hard way and the easy way, choose the easy way." This is not to say that challenges should be avoided, but rather that the Universe conspires to give you what you want with as little resistance as possible. That's just the way it works. If you are not experiencing life in an effortless manner, you need to consider the possibility that you have created blocks that are standing in the way of energy's easy-flowing nature.

I must stress that THIS IS NOT A BAD THING; THIS IS A GIFT. Instead of feeling frustrated that life is difficult, you must be grateful for the clarity of the signal telling you that there is a block EXACTLY WHERE YOU ARE. You don't need to guess or search around in the dark; the block is RIGHT there in the "hard place." Most people focus their energy on being frustrated by the difficulty or on avoiding it altogether. As a result, they miss the golden opportunity to be done with it once and for all. Once you work out the blockage in the energy, you will again experience life in its more natural form—effortless.

Let's focus for a minute on being blocked. Blockages contain significant life lessons. Imperative in all spiritual growth is to fully commit to dealing with the blocks. This can be challenging and sometimes painful. That's

> *"Security is mostly a superstition. It does not exist in nature, nor do the children of men as a whole experience it. Avoiding danger is no safer in the long run than outright exposure. Life is either a daring adventure or nothing."*
>
> —Helen Keller

okay. You might actually feel as though you are going crazy, but that's a good sign, a sign that things are on the brink of changing. Because change is unpredictable, it's scary. Remember, the mind doesn't like unpredictable, so avoiding change becomes the mind's strategy for keeping us safe. The paradox is that avoiding change is actually more dangerous because it keeps us stuck in a cycle that denies our growth. This goes against the reality of nature. We are all either growing or withering.

Change

If we recognize and accept that nothing in nature remains static, including human beings, it will be easier to accept that it is normal for life to change all the time. This, in turn, means that it is completely normal to feel the apprehension and fear associated with impending change. What is really important is to remember that feeling this apprehension and fear is normal, but that it should not stop the process. If we allow these feelings to stop the process, we have created a block in the natural flow and order of the Universe. This is what causes the "mixed signals" we send

to the Universe when trying to get what we want. Energetic blocks arise when we consciously or unconsciously arrest the natural process of change and evolution that is occurring all the time.

Let me say it one more time. Change is scary, but change is natural. Remaining constant or trying to create a comfort zone that never changes is actually counterproductive to our design and will be a major source of our suffering in life. Sometimes we need outside help such as counselling or personal development courses and books to deal with our blocks, challenges and changes. Remember, this is normal. It doesn't make us weird or unusual. In fact, we are doing ourselves a disservice by ignoring our opportunities to make changes. Change is the very foundation of growth and is absolutely necessary if we are to continue evolving.

Somewhere along the line, most of us got hurt in the process of changing and so we concluded that change was risky business. Let's face it, if we really stop and think about it, just living is dangerous. Anything could happen when we walk out the door. My theory is that, since we can't really control how we are going to die—whether while crossing the street or parachuting from a plane—we might as well live the fullest lives possible. After all, the view from the sky is usually magnificent.

Rather than avoiding change, we'd benefit more by creating strategies to help deal with the apprehension that

usually accompanies change. We can start by recognizing that change is absolutely essential and normal for all things in nature. This means that we are not going crazy or revealing some hidden weirdness. We are not the first generation in history to experience fear, discomfort or pain. What's so interesting is that, often, people are actually very ready for change and also particularly bored in their current situation. But change is hard. I know it is. If you find it's really hard, get some help.

Let's think of the child who is ready to read all by herself. She knows all the letters and sounds. She wants to understand those strange words that she sees all around. Intellectually, she is ready for the challenge and her mind is well equipped to process the information. Emotionally, she is also ready because in her is a deep desire to progress and create relationships with other kids at her level. But there is one problem. She doesn't know how to read and she doesn't know how to figure it out on her own. She gets frustrated. She keeps trying things that don't work and she still can't read those stupid words. She is getting really mad now. She feels like she is going crazy. Her emotions betray her and she is angry or sad. She begins to doubt that she will ever be able to read and starts to think about giving up. What's the point if she is always going to feel so badly about it? Then a teacher shows up. Someone who already knows how to read and, better yet, knows how to teach others to

read. This teacher shows the child how to read, and in an instant her entire world changes. She can read. All of a sudden, beautiful words begin to emerge everywhere. The child is ecstatic, joyful and happy. The child will never be the same again because she will never *unlearn* how to read.

It is very important to notice that in this scenario the teacher is the catalyst—and an absolute necessity. Without the teacher, the child may have remained stuck indefinitely. It is no different in your life now. If you are stuck, you probably need a teacher to help guide you through the process. As an adult, our teachers take on many forms—a therapist, minister, friend, elder and sometimes even a child. Our culture has placed a certain stigma on these "teachers," concluding that only weak, weird or crazy people would ever really need someone like this. You probably already know that I am going to say that this is pure hogwash. The reality is that if you are feeling stuck in your life, then you probably need a teacher of some kind. Get the help you need and get over your story about needing it.

> *"Just when the caterpillar thought the world was over, it became a butterfly."*
> —Anonymous

Now the stage is finally set for you to start "doing" things. A quick review of your checklist should reveal that you have completed the following steps:

- Decided on your finish line (Deliberate Creation)
- Created your energetic reality by experiencing the feeling of reaching that finish line (Law of Attraction)
- Stated your guiding values and principles to help assist you when life happens quickly

But where to start and how to know when you are taking inspired action vs. ego-action? Years ago, when I was doing some high-level corporate strategic planning, I developed a little acronym for helping with just that. I call it the SMASHing system and it has always helped me clarify the things I am doing in my life. Once you have a finish line in mind, it is crucial to have a plan to help get you there. Think of it as a map. You know where you are now and you know where you want to go. Having a route in mind is usually very helpful.

Caution

At this point, it's very important to remember that while your route may be excellent and well thought out, it is not the *only* route from where you are now to where you are going. Always, always, always remember that there is a most straightforward path and you may not yet have identified it. You must trust in this process. If you get too attached to "your way," you may find yourself in the land of difficulty and frustration instead of ease and flowing. My rule is to always "pay attention to what gets my attention," as that is a very trustworthy way of following my "right path."

A route map or plan is an excellent way to fill your days with inspired actions. After all, if you are in pursuit of something you desire, you are full of inspiration. If you take your finish line and break it down into four or five smaller more manageable goals, you will be well on your way to creating a whole bunch of inspired actions. The best way I know to ensure that your goals are robust enough to get you from A to B is to apply the SMASHing system to them.

SMASHing stands for:
- **S**ustainable
- **M**easurable
- **A**ctionable
- **S**ingle-Minded
- **H**armonized

Sustainable

Does your goal or vision stand the test of time, or is it something that can be accomplished within minutes? Being sustainable means that your goals will be able to inspire you and guide you as you move towards your finish line. Your goals are stepping stones that contribute to the overall big picture of your finish line. Therefore, their timeliness should correspond to an appropriate length of time related to the overall time expected to arrive at your finish line. For example, as I write this book, my overall finish line is to publish the book by February 2007.

One of my goals is to write the first draft by Labour Day. This goal is sustainable and keeps me working on a daily basis to achieve it. A poor choice of goals may have been to write the first chapter by Labour Day. This would have only taken me one day to accomplish and would have left me without a goal on the following day.

Measurable

You must be able to assess whether or not you achieve your goals. In a sense, your goals are mini finish lines along your path. These mini finish lines are only valuable if you can quickly ascertain your success by measuring against a benchmark or set point. In the Feedback Loop of Life, these are the minor adjustments that allow you to alter your course based on the daily feedback you get about the actions you are taking. If you pay close enough attention to these metrics, you can quickly respond to the feedback from the Universe as to the direction of the most straightforward path to your goal. Using my example of writing the first draft by Labour Day, you can plainly see the measurement I am using to define my success. The date of Labour Day gives me a mini finish line, a performance point, and I will be able to say "yes" or "no" definitively.

Actionable

To be actionable, a goal must contain a verb. In other words, you must clearly define what you will DO with your

time. Goals that lack verbs do not direct you to definitive action. Again using my example, you can see that the verb in my goal is "to write." Therefore, I know that if I am not writing, chances are my draft isn't going to be done in time. When I am feeling a little foggy, I still know what to do—write. A goal of "a finished first draft by Labour Day" is poorly worded because it lacks an action verb.

Single-Minded

Your goals must have clarity of purpose. Too often, I meet people whose goals are wishy-washy and vague. They are not compelling and, as a result, rarely get achieved. Having a clear purpose provides you the impetus for action. Again using my example, it is very clear: I must write the first draft by Labour Day. Defining "first draft" dictates to me exactly what is expected. I could have said, "Begin writing the book by Labour Day," but that could be misconstrued and appear very overwhelming. By staying focused and clear about my goal, I am able to take actions each and every day to move towards it.

Harmonized

Your goals absolutely must be harmonized with your guiding values and principles. If you are out of alignment in this area, you will experience great difficulty in your day-to-day actions. Remember, the goal is to continue moving towards the finish line. Therefore, your goals must be in

harmony with your overall finish line. Using my example again, I can easily demonstrate how it is harmonized. You see, one of my guiding principles is "to grow by taking on challenges outside my comfort zone." This is my first book. I had a million reasons NOT to write it and at the top of my list was "I have never done it before." But, by listening to my inner guidance and staying committed to my values, I was able to overcome my own apprehension and finish this book.

The SMASHing system ensures that the actions we take are congruent with our finish line. It also allows us to take small measurements along the way to determine if we are on track in the big picture. This is the part of the feedback loop that allows for minor adjustments, the part that allows us to change some of the things we are doing in hope of altering our outcome. This only works if we have not yet reached the finish line and are still in the realm of temporary reality. This minor feedback loop allows us to measure the efficacy of our goals and to understand any major shortfalls as we head towards the realm of physical reality. That is why it is so important that our goals be measurable—so they can serve a useful purpose in helping us stay closest to the most straightforward path. Paying attention to the minor feedback along the way is

> *"Go confidently in the direction of your dreams! Live the life you've imagined."*
> —Henry David Thoreau

like listening for the whispers from God instead of waiting for Her to smack us with a cosmic two-by-four.

SMASH IT

Use this worksheet to help you create a SMASHing goal.

Write your goal here: _____

_____

Sustainable: _____

Measurable: _____

Actionable: _____

Single-Minded: _____

Harmonized: _____

Making Babies

One thing that stops a lot of people is becoming completely overwhelmed by the sheer size of their vision or goals. If from time to time you find yourself in this group, it may be helpful for you to learn how to make babies of your goals. This is basically the process of breaking down your goals until you feel comfortable with their manageability. The ultimate size of the goal is different for everyone, but the process is the same. First and foremost, all babies must pass the SMASHing test. Second, the "sum of the babies" must equal the larger "parent" goal. The process is easiest to define using a simple example.

Parent Goal: To eat a healthy diet by New Year's Day

First, we need to ensure that our parent goal passes the SMASHing test. Assuming that the goal is made on July 1, it is definitely sustainable. The date of New Year's Day gives it a measure. The verb "to eat" is definitely an action. The goal is focused and single-minded and is harmonized with the individual's commitment to lead a healthy life. However, the goal is still overwhelming because it really isn't clear exactly what to do on each day between now and New Year's Day. Making babies will help clarify the goal.

Baby Goals:
- To eat 10 servings of fruits and vegetables every day
- To reduce coffee consumption to 1 cup per day
- To limit sugar consumption to parties and special events
- To eat only organic food

Each of the baby goals passes our SMASHing test, and together they easily add up to a "healthy diet." This could be the final breakdown of goals in this situation. However, if any of the baby goals still feel overwhelming, then another round of making babies can occur. This has a cascading effect in that each generation of goals can be broken down into more and more babies until you are literally left with a daily action plan of things to do that are direct descendants

of your big-picture finish line. This is a great way to ensure that you are moving towards your finish line in the best way you know how. When you are ascertaining whether or not a baby goal is sustainable in the SMASHing system, you need to keep in mind how many generations of goals you have made. A baby goal might be sustainable in the 1-2 day mark if all the other goals in that generation are of that stature. In our example, you could make another generation of goal babies in this way:

New Parent Goal:
  • To reduce coffee consumption to 1 cup per day

Next Generation of Babies:
  • Reduce current coffee consumption to 3 cups per day by September 30
  • Refrain from drinking coffee out of paper cups to discourage over-consumption
  • Drink only organic coffee
  • Replace coffee consumption with herbal tea

You can plainly see how each generation of goal babies gets more and more specific and easy to accomplish. In this way, you are able to take on even the biggest goals and break them down until you feel comfortable with the action plan. The next thing you can do is transfer this action plan to your daily calendar.

Inspired "To Do" Lists

It is possible to fill each and every item on your "to do" list with an action that is inspired directly from the big picture of your finish line. Making goal babies is an excellent way to move confidently towards your finish line. You must start at the very top with a clear and concise picture of your finish line. Then, you begin by making the first generation of goal babies. I recommend limiting each generation to four or five babies; otherwise, the plan gets too diluted. It can take as many as four to six generations of goal babies to get down to the tactical level of action lists. You will know it when you get there.

Once you are at the generation of the "to do" list, you simply transfer your action items to a 12-month calendar. I recommend using a 12-month calendar because many of your actions will be recurring (daily, weekly, monthly) and it helps to lay the whole thing out so you can see the path you have created. Once you have filled in the entire 12-month calendar with all your little goal babies, you will see that you have finally removed all the guesswork from life. Your calendar dictates exactly what you should be focusing on and when you should be doing it because it came directly from the big picture of your finish line. Gone are the days of dragging your feet feeling overwhelmed by all your goals and the things you have to do. Your babies do the work for you by keeping you in line with your big picture.

Caution

It is very easy to overlook the things that support you in achieving your dreams. Things like rest, relaxation and rejuvenation are as important as any "official" item on your action list. You must also include these types of actions in your 12-month planning calendar so you can see where it is you will recharge your batteries and ensure your energy levels remain adequate to do the things you want to do. I have a client who literally schedules every book she reads, every run she takes and even how many social functions she will attend every month. In this way, she is able to keep a balance between living the life of her dreams and maintaining a high enough energy level to reach the finish line. Obviously, life doesn't always go according to plan, but *having* a balanced plan is the key to understanding the give-and-take nature of your actions. Having a good plan allows you to feel confident in the actions you are taking every day because you understand exactly how they fit into the big picture of your dreams.

Throwing It Away

Now throw all of this away. What? How can I suggest throwing the whole plan away after you spent so much time crafting it? Well, I'm not suggesting that you throw the plan itself away, but you must—and I stress MUST—throw away your attachment to it. You will inevitably become attached to your plan because you have laboured

to create it. You have spent a lot of time checking the "SMASH-ability" of your goals and rigorously readjusting them. You have spent a lot of time making the perfect babies and ensuring that absolutely nothing gets left out as you move towards the big picture of your finish line. But being attached to your plan will prevent you from seeing the signs and hearing the whispers as to where you need to alter your course along the path to your goal.

Remember, the actions we take in temporary reality are meant to move us from our energetic reality to our physical reality. This temporary reality is where the Universe catches up with us and helps us create the physical manifestation of the energetic reality we have already created. The Universe already knows the most straightforward path that will bring about this physical reality. We have to trust the Universe on this one. Your plan may be good, but you might not have all the information to declare it the "most straightforward" path. You must pay attention to the signs along the way and adjust your actions according to the minor feedback you get on a daily basis. You may find yourself moving more quickly or more slowly than originally anticipated. If this happens to you, trust it. Go with the flow. Remember that the apprehension or anxiety you might be feeling is just your mind trying to keep you safe. The path from energetic reality to physical reality is not a linear one. The Universe isn't linear. Absolutely anything is possible, but you must have faith in the process.

In the Feedback Loop of Life, this is the little section where you get to change your actions in an effort to reach your finish line. This minor feedback comes straight from the Universe based on what you said you wanted when you deliberately created the finish line in the

> *"Do one thing every day that scares you."*
> —Eleanor Roosevelt

first place. Here you must pay attention to what gets your attention in order to be able to clearly see your most straightforward path. You must let go of your attachment to your plan and have faith in the Universal Laws. They work every time, no exceptions. You must adjust your plan and continue to take actions that are inspired from the big picture of your finish line.

As you move towards your finish line, your lessons and opportunities will show up as big challenges and confronting situations. This is the physical manifestation of your energetic blocks and what, literally, stands between you and what you want. The most straightforward path to your finish line contains shortcuts that will catapult you directly into the life of your dreams. However, you must first eliminate any energy blocks from the path.

The process of clearing blocks is similar to a video game where you must get past the obstacles in order to progress to the next level. Think of your energy blocks as obstacles in your "video game of life." If you understand what the obstacle is and are able to access the right tool

to deal with it, you can eliminate the obstacle for good and move on to the next level in the game. The Universe knows exactly which obstacles stand in your way, and it will continually present you with the opportunity to deal with and eliminate that obstacle once and for all. Your greatest challenges contain your greatest opportunities because, once handled, they allow you to take the shortcut on your most straightforward path to your finish line. This process also makes you stronger because, once gained, you can never unlearn the lessons that come from your biggest challenges.

Look, therefore, for things in your life that scare you, confront you, challenge you and even anger you. Releasing the negative energy surrounding these events will clear them from your life forever.

> *"People who say it cannot be done should not interrupt those who are doing it."*
> —Author Unknown

The First Is the Worst

When in the midst of your process, it will be helpful to remember that the first time trying anything new is always the worst. Everything gets better as we gain experience and knowledge. Remembering this will be key as you move towards your finish line. As you begin to take on your obstacles, you will gain proficiency

and confidence with it. This means that clearing your energy blocks and eliminating your obstacles actually gets easier and easier. If you commit to making it a habit to deal with your obstacles, you will move more quickly towards your finish line. Every new challenge you take on becomes an awesome opportunity to accelerate your growth. Each and every time you do it you become better at it, and soon you are able to take on much more and get there that much quicker. Knowing this, you can allow yourself to fully experience each and every thing that happens and understand that it's all good, no matter what it is.

"Never confuse a single defeat with a final defeat."

—F. Scott Fitzgerald

chapter 5

HAVE – THE PHYSICAL REALITY

"We are what we think. All that we are arises with our thoughts. With our thoughts, we make our world."

—Buddha

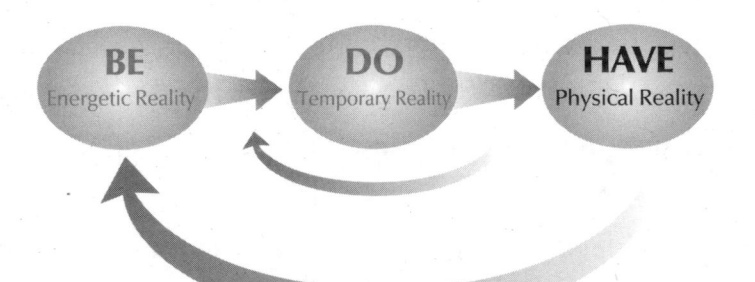

This chapter is my favourite because it covers the area where I have experienced the most growth. Namely, accepting reality as perfect, exactly as it appears. This task is not always easy, especially if our current reality is painful or unpleasant. But it cannot be

any other way. For if it could, it would. What we have is exactly what we have attracted. What we have is exactly perfect for us at any given moment in time. There are no mistakes. Consciously or unconsciously, we have attracted the present moment.

If what you currently have is NOT what you want, then you have to understand that the Universe is giving you valuable feedback that a disconnect between your input (BE) and your output (HAVE) has occurred. If your physical reality does not match the energetic reality you were trying to create, you have glaring evidence that there is a blockage in your energy and that the signals you have been sending to the Universe may have been mixed. This is not a bad thing. It is simply course-corrective feedback. Your built-in feedback mechanism is giving you all the guidance you need to create what you want. Thus, it would be of great benefit to start viewing this feedback as a very, very *good* thing.

With this feedback mechanism, there is no need to speculate as to whether you are doing it right. Physical reality shows you that if you do NOT have what you want, then you have been sending the Universe mixed signals. Period. With this information, you can start to look objectively at your signals to determine where the hold-up occurred. Once the problem has been identified, you can handle the energy blockage, clear the pathway and repeat the process until you have exactly what you want, exactly the way you want it.

Please note that once you can see that you do NOT have your desired goal or "finish line," you absolutely must go back to the input level and change your energy (BE). If at this point in the process you simply try to change your actions, you will only manifest more and more of the same result. The only way to avoid this insanity is to recognize that a mix-up occurred in your process and that this problem must be solved at the energetic level of creation and attraction. It cannot be solved at the physical level of "doing."

Failure

When what we get is NOT what we wanted, we often label the result a "failure." The definition of failure is "act of failing; a proving unsuccessful; lack of success." Simply put, failure means that we were not successful in getting something we wanted. That's it. So what? Culturally, however, we have been taught to absorb much more than this about failure. We have been taught that failure is shameful because it somehow indicates our inadequacy. We have learned, through receiving the criticism of those who have meant the most to us, that failure is painful. And because, in an effort to avoid further suffering, the mind loves to dwell in the pain of the distant past, we have deduced that the risk of failure isn't worth the reward of success.

Another look at the dictionary gives an alternate meaning for "failure." It also means "running short; insufficiency: *as in failure of crops*." Perhaps this definition shows us the

root of our associating failure with inadequacy. However, nowhere in the dictionary can I find a meaning that associates failure with the insufficiency of the person who is trying something—only the insufficiency of the results.

Failure is not judgment; it is feedback. That's it. There is nothing more to it. We either got what we wanted or we didn't. Failure doesn't come with a judgment card that gives us a pass or fail as a human being. Failure is feedback! If we stop lamenting our failures and using them as proof of our worthlessness, we can finally be free to use the valuable information contained in these experiences. What we do not get in life contains the clues as to what stands between us and what we really want. Our failures are the key to our actually being able to create and manifest anything we want. We simply need to look at the difference between what we wanted and what we got. We should be able to easily identify the limiting belief or sabotaging effort that blocked the reception of what we wanted. We do this for a number of reasons, the primary one being that we are tied to old belief patterns we created about ourselves during childhood. Typically these beliefs have to

> *"We learn wisdom from failure much more than from success. We often discover what will do by finding out what will not do. And probably he who never made a mistake never made a discovery."*
> —Samuel Smiles

do with being unlovable, unworthy or otherwise inadequate. If we look at our failures with objective eyes, we will be able to recognize these belief patterns and will finally be free to work through them and get them out of the way.

It's All Good

Everything that happens is perfect. Everything that happens *to* us has been created and attracted *by* us. The Universe simply delivers what we order. As the earlier chapters indicated, we are free to order exactly what we want. We can literally place an order for the life we want and, according to Universal Law, it will be delivered to us. It's not a trick. The secret, however, is understanding that if we do NOT get what we want, then we, ourselves, are responsible for having attracted that outcome too. Results don't come from somewhere else, somewhere "out there." They come from us. The first step to clearing what is blocking what we want is to accept responsibility for creating those blocks in the first place. Before we can choose a different way of being and get different results, we must be conscious of our role in the process. Awareness is the first step.

I recognize that this viewpoint can be difficult for some people, especially those who have suffered unpleasant or even awful circumstances. Let me be clear: I am not saying that your circumstances are your "fault." I am not saying that you did anything "wrong" or that you are "bad." What I am saying is that, at some level, you are attracting the unpleasant

or awful things you are experiencing. And often you need help to stop this pattern. The physical reality of your situation is crying out to you to identify and halt the destructive energy. A great place to start changing this pattern is by doing all of the exercises in this book. You can also visit my website www.GinaML.com for more resources. If you are having trouble, you might consider finding a therapist, counselor, minister, teacher, relative, book or course to help you release any negative energy. We all must take responsibility for helping ourselves, and if this means getting outside help then that's perfectly fine!

Shift in the Now

Now is the only time we really have. Past and future are simply illusions created by the mind to give it context in this physical world. Think about it: There really isn't any "place" where the past exists nor is there any "place" where the future exists. All we have is now, now, now—a series of moments strung together. The power to alter our experience exists only in the present moment.

You can use this understanding when you experience a failure. At the point in time that the failure occurs, you have a choice to make. You can either use the information to alter something about your energy or you can choose to lament your failure and indulge the negative energy that you have been taught to create. Either way, the choice is yours and yours alone. Either way, the choice occurs in the present

moment and the opportunity for the choice does not linger or wait. You have only "the now" wherein to make your choice. You can use your present moments wisely and choose to see the lessons in the feedback you are continually receiving.

Expectations

Any discontent we feel about our circumstances has absolutely everything to do with our expectations. It is our expectations, not our actual circumstances, that cause unhappiness. Again, life is the way it is because it is the way it is. And it is perfect exactly as it is. If we experience discontent with the way it is, then we must recognize that this discontent is created by our minds because the physical reality doesn't align with our minds' expectations of how it should be. This "should" is the root cause of our unhappiness. If we can release the "should," we will experience freedom and happiness. Rather than try in vain to control all the external circumstances, all we have to do is let go of the "should" and all discontent will instantly vanish. Poof!

From time to time, people have been known to cut me off in traffic. This used to upset me because I held the expectation that no one should *ever* cut me off in traffic. It used to really bother me. One day it dawned on me that the reason it was bothering me was because I was engaging in my expectation. I shifted my expectation and, miraculously, the other drivers stopped bothering me, even though they continued to cut me off! I realized that I can't control them,

only my reaction to the situation. By the way, I now use these types of situations as signals. If I notice that I am judging other drivers, it usually informs me that I am indulging some low-energy emotion. I use my feelings as a signal to shift my vibration into something higher, like love or acceptance. At this point, the "bad drivers" usually disappear.

100-0

Another way to express this new view is to live life at 100-0, where you commit to giving 100% of your effort at all times while expecting absolutely nothing in return. This is particularly powerful in relationships. You give 100% to the relationship and expect 0% in return from your partner. If your partner is also living this way, then she or he is giving you 100% while expecting 0% from you. It is a complete win-win situation with both partners giving and receiving perfectly. Think about your own relationships. Do you give 100% or do you hold back because you expect the other person to give or do something for you? Do you expect things from others and then get frustrated when those things don't materialize? We need to recognize that it is simply our expectation that is causing the upset, not the actual circumstances. It is *always* the expectation.

> "When we are no longer able to change a situation, we are challenged to change ourselves."
>
> —Viktor Frankl

Meaning Machines

The human mind is a "meaning-creating machine." It loves to create stories. In fact, it needs stories to explain and understand the physical world. Therefore, the mind is always making up stories. This, in and of itself, is not a problem. The problem arises when we begin to believe our stories as the only reality or "truth" in the world. We must recognize that our minds create all the meaning about the events that happen to us. There is no "truth" about these events, but rather only the meaning our minds give them.

Imagine meeting a friend for lunch. You are waiting at the restaurant and your friend is late. Instantly, your mind creates a story, or a meaning, about this event. Let's say your mind decides that your friend is late because she doesn't value your time. This makes you angry, and now you feel slighted by your friend. The longer you wait, the more upset you become as your mind spins this elaborate story. By the time your friend arrives, you can barely contain your upset. Upon arriving, your friend apologizes and explains that she stopped to help an elderly lady carry her groceries and this caused her to be late.

This type of reaction happens all the time. The stories and meanings you attach to events in your life are not "the truth," but rather what your mind has made up about those events. In fact, these stories or "truths" are the cause of most of the disharmony in our world today. Consider how

> *"The real voyage of discovery consists not in seeing new landscapes, but in having new eyes."*
>
> —Marcel Proust

many wars are waged based on "truth." There are always multiple stories that describe the exact same event.

One thing you can do when noticing that you are upset is to try to understand your story. The first thing to ask yourself is: "Do I know for sure that this is true?" You will usually find that you cannot be 100% sure that your story is the "true" story. If you find yourself stuck on your version of a story, try making up some alternate stories to explain the exact same event. I recommend choosing five different stories with the following themes:

- Silly story – Your friend was late because her trapeze practice ran late.
- Dramatic story – Your friend was late because she rescued a cat from a burning building.
- Magical story – Your friend was late because her unicorn had to eat before flying her over.
- Touching story – Your friend was late because she was reading a story to children at the local daycare.
- Inspiring story – Your friend was late because she was marching in a peace rally.

Once you have compared the five stories and considered the possibility of each one, you should be able to see that there is no "truth." This should illustrate that your story is also not "the truth" and you now have the power to unchoose

your story. You can detach from the meaning and get back into living your life, being happy in the present moment exactly as it is happening.

Life Is a Mirror

The things we experience on the outside are simply a reflection of what is happening on the inside. Our lives are mirrors of our inner world. If we accept that we are ultimately responsible for attracting everything that happens to us, then our experience is completely reflective of the energy we are putting out into the world. Remember that, according to Quantum Theory, we are simply energy and everything around us is also energy. This means that our physical experience is merely a manifestation of our inner energy. In fact, our lives are perfect little mirrors and they reflect back exactly what is happening on every level— without exception.

This is great news if you know how to use a mirror. The first thing you need to do is look at the mirror and understand that it is not "reality in itself," but rather a reflection of reality. What you see in the mirror is not the "real thing," so it would be futile to try to change the picture in the mirror. You understand that if you want the picture in the mirror to be different, then you must change the image that the mirror is reflecting. This means that you must change your inner world if you ever want your outer world to look different.

Inside-Out

In other words, mirrors are not to blame for the pictures they reflect. Imagine waking up one day with really bad hair. You can see how bad your hair is by looking in the mirror. Now imagine that you start yelling at the mirror and demanding that it show you different hair. Your upset is coming from your expectation that the mirror should reflect your "good hair" simply because you want it to. Under this expectation, you get upset and blame the mirror for continuing to reflect your bad hair. Obviously, the only way to change the picture in the mirror is to actually do something about your hair. Recognizing that the mirror is a reflection of reality gives us the freedom to choose. You can choose to fix your hair, thus also changing the picture in the mirror, or you can choose to do nothing about your hair, recognizing that the mirror will continue to display your bad hair. Either way, the choice is yours and there is much freedom in understanding this choice.

This principle applies to the rest of life in exactly the same way. In the Feedback Loop of Life what we HAVE is "the mirror." So, in your life, what you have on the outside is a reflection of who you are BEING on the inside. If you are unhappy with what you see in your life, then it is absolutely futile to try to change something on the outside. You must go to the source of the image (who you are being) and change it on the inside; then you can look to the reflection to determine if your change was adequate.

You must look to the reflection for feedback on the changes you have made on the inside. If the reflection is what you want, you have succeeded; if the reflection is NOT what you want, you simply need to look to see what is out of place and then go inward to change it.

In my workshops, I actually give every participant a little mirror to remind her or him of the simplicity of the built-in feedback mechanism available to each of us at all times. By looking at life on the outside, in the mirror, we can determine what needs to be changed on the inside to alter the picture we are seeing.

USING THE MIRROR PRINCIPLE

This technique is so simple and allows you to change virtually anything in your life. Here's how to use it:

1. Identify what is causing you to be upset.
2. Change your language to "I."
3. Deal with the issue.

1. Identify the Upset

It is easy to spot the cause of your upset—it is that one thing you want to change or that circumstance (or person) you want to eliminate. It is usually the thing you blame for your life not being the way you want it to be. You typically place this blame on something external. For example, you might find yourself saying, "If only my boyfriend treated me with respect, then I would be happy." It is obvious to

you that your unhappiness is the fault of your boyfriend and something he is or isn't doing. Now, however, you have to shift into realizing that he doesn't cause you to be unhappy. *You* do. Or better put, the *choices* you make are causing you to be unhappy. Your boyfriend is simply a reflection of your inability to treat yourself with respect. In other words, don't shoot the messenger! Instead, you need to be grateful for the clarity you are being shown.

2. Change Your Language

This is very powerful. By changing your language to "I," you are taking responsibility for your own upset. This gives you the power necessary to change your energy. In the example above, changing your language means that your statement becomes, "If only I would treat myself with respect, then I would be happy." Notice that the onus is now on you to change your behaviour. There is no longer anyone else to blame for your situation. You now turn your focus inward, where it is possible to recreate and change the picture that is being reflected in your mirror.

3. Deal with the Issue

Once you have refocused the responsibility back on yourself, you are finally able to alter your energy around the issue. This may be simple or challenging depending on what the issue means to you and how elaborate your story

is about it. Remember that your mind has created this story to protect you from some perceived harm, so it may be challenging to reverse the belief. However, the power once again rests with your choice. You can choose to delve deeper into the issue and look for the answer, or you can choose to ignore it and turn the other way. Delving deeper might mean you need someone's help to see it a different way. Your life will reflect back to you exactly what you choose to do. Your physical experience will mirror your energetic reality. Like in a video game, if you master the obstacle, you will be able to move to the next level of life. If not, you will spend your life running from or avoiding the obstacle, which is a colossal waste of your energy.

MIRROR, MIRROR

1. **Identify what is causing you to be upset.** Look for people or situations that cause you to be upset.

   _____

2. **Change your language to "I."** In the statement above, replace all references to others with references to yourself in the first person.

   _____

3. **Deal with the issue.** List three different ways you can resolve the real issue.

   _____

Pay Attention to What Gets Your Attention

The easiest way to determine what part of your reflection isn't working for you is to notice what gets your attention. Note that what gets your attention might not get someone else's attention. Whatever it is, you are noticing it because it is important to you and your reason for being on this earth. For example, you might notice something because you could be the key to solving some major world problem or the catalyst for massive change. What we notice is as unique to each of us as our fingerprints. So, we would be wise to focus our efforts on the things that get our attention the most, as these situations often contain our biggest opportunities for growth and contribution.

> *"What we are familiar with we cease to see."*
>
> —Anaïs Nin

The Law of Allowing

It is easy for most people to agree that we need to be deliberate and conscious in creating a vision or "finish line" for ourselves (the Law of Deliberate Creation). Likewise, most people don't have much trouble understanding that we get what we attract because we are an energetic creature subject to energetic laws (the Law of Attraction). What makes the Law of Allowing the hardest of the Universal Laws to accept is that it requires complete surrender because it means that we must allow for exactly what is happening to happen exactly as it is. You may have noticed that human

beings don't do very well in the category of "surrender." As a whole, we are mainly control freaks who perceive surrender as a vulnerability or weakness. This is why we experience so much trouble with the concept of God; having faith requires a complete surrender and this is hard for people.

The human mind is consumed with creating little "realms of control" that offer a certain level of comfort on a daily basis. The goal of the mind is to remain in the realm of control so as to avoid the perils of life on Earth. If we begin to travel outside of the mind's realm of control, the mind will have great difficulty predicting the outcome and our ultimate safety. Surrendering usually falls into the category of "risky behaviour" because there is no element of control while we are surrendering. Surrender is the complete opposite of control because it means to relinquish control. The Law of Allowing states that we must yield to the Universal Laws and allow experience to manifest itself accordingly.

We must allow what is happening to us to happen. We must also allow what is happening to others to happen. It's not that we don't take action, but rather that we detach from the meaning and significance the mind has created about what happens. Your path is your path. Another's path is another's path. When you can fully accept this, you will have mastered the Law of Allowing. It seems difficult to accept something like war or hatred. Recognize that your experience of war or hatred is merely a reflection of what is going on at an energetic level, either inside of you or

collectively as the human race. Perhaps the experience of war or hatred is what is really needed in order to facilitate a massive shift at the energetic level.

The bottom line is that everything is happening exactly and perfectly according to Universal Law. The Universe doesn't make mistakes. Energy can only follow Universal Law. If circumstances are unpleasant or even atrocious, then we must accept that this is simply a reflection of unpleasant or atrocious energy inside of us. The Law of Allowing is about understanding and trusting that everything is being reflected perfectly—without exception. When we are able to allow life to unfold without resistance, we experience great freedom, as the burden of discontent is finally lifted from our shoulders. In your own life, you will experience this as being able to observe life as an unfolding of a series of events without expectation. You will be able to marvel in the magnificence of the Universe and her immutable laws. You will be able to see your own reflection and adjust your energy according to your vision.

> *"A thing is complete when you can let it be."*
> —Gita Bellin

Life Is a Cycle

It sounds cliché to say that life is a journey, but it really is. The Feedback Loop of Life is merely a cycle that is repeated indefinitely while we are here on Earth. Basically, we want

something, we do some things to get it and then we either get what we wanted or we do not. Then, we repeat the cycle. Over and over again until our time on Earth is done. The question remains as to whether or not we will use the built-in feedback mechanism available to us to change our way of being so we can effect different outcomes.

Our results are a perfect reflection of the exact pattern of energy we have created. If we do NOT have what we want, then we have the power to choose a different way of being. This different way of being will allow for a different outcome. We can repeatedly change our way of being until our physical reality matches our intended energetic reality. Until these match, we have work to do. This work will come in the form of lessons and obstacles. All these challenges serve to facilitate our spiritual growth, because we are, after all, just blobs of energy experiencing the physical world. There is no "right way" or "wrong way," only the unfolding of events according to Universal Law. There are no tricks or secrets, only straightforward principles that govern all the energy in the universe. If we do NOT have what we want, then there is a disconnect. We get all the feedback we ever need to alter our physical reality. It comes down to our choices. We can choose to use the feedback or not, but in the end we are responsible

"Here is a test to find out whether your mission in life is complete... If you're alive, it isn't."

—Richard Bach

for the consequences of that choice. If you ever wonder whether or not your work on Earth is finished, just ask yourself one question: "Am I still alive?" If so, your work is not finished! Period.

chapter 6

THINGS THAT HELP

"There is nothing I can tell you that you do not already know. There is no question that you can ask me that you yourself cannot answer. You have just forgotten."

—David Littlewood

This chapter is dedicated to supporting your efforts to get the most out of your life. There are things you can do to help make your journey easier and more enjoyable. You aren't obligated to do any of them, but experience has shown that these strategies help significantly to change your energetic state. When you are feeling down, it is an indication that you are vibrating at a low energetic level. Knowing how to raise your energy can significantly increase your enjoyment in life.

It is also important to remember that the Law of Attraction is governed by your energy, so if you really want to attract amazing things into your life, it is wise to keep your energy levels as high as possible for as long as possible.

You will find that life is much more enjoyable and you'll simply feel better when your focus is on maintaining a higher vibration. The physical world will reflect back to you the positive state of your inner energetic world. Remember, this is an inside-out process. If you focus your efforts on managing your inner world, your outside world will be a direct physical manifestation. It is fairly easy to tell when you are vibrating at a low level. The quickest way is to look around at your physical world for feedback. If you are feeling bad, sad, upset, angry or any other low-energy emotion, then chances are you need to raise your energetic vibration.

Handles

Those of you who are scientifically inclined will remember Newton's Third Law of Thermodynamics, which states that "an object in motion tends to stay in motion unless acted upon by an outside force, whereas an object at rest tends to stay at rest unless acted upon by an outside force." This absolutely applies to human beings as energetic creatures, because our energetic state is governed by this law as well. Simply put, if we are maintaining a low-vibration energy level, we will continue to do so until "acted upon by an outside force," which means we must change the vibration.

When we are low, it is common to feel as though we are spiralling downward and that things are getting worse and worse. Don't fret; this is simply the Law of Attraction in

action. We attract what we focus on, so if we focus on negative energy, we will continue to attract more negative energy. It seems like a vicious cycle with no apparent way out. The most powerful way to change the vibration is to choose a different one. This isn't always easy to do, especially when we feel as though we are falling downward.

A powerful metaphor to help us shift out of this downward spiral is to think of grabbing on to a handle. As we grab the handle, our decline halts immediately. At this point, we are free to use the handle to begin our climb back up to a higher vibrational state. However, we must make the choice to use what help is readily available to us. The handle will not grab us; we must choose to grab it. As always, the choice and the responsibility are ours.

Gratitude

Gratitude is, by far, the most powerful handle to grab when life seems desperate. Gratitude has the power to immediately reverse any negative energy. When we shift into gratitude, we have literally flipped an energetic

> "You cannot be grateful and hateful at the same time."
> —Gina Mollicone-Long

switch. Given that gratitude only resides in the present moment, we will feel an instant shift in our energy level.

Studies have shown that an attitude of gratitude actually affects the physical world immediately, and this includes the human body. Dr. Masaru Emoto is famous for his "Hidden

Messages in Water"[2] experiments that have shown the effect of gratitude on water molecules. When placed in the presence of loving and grateful energy, the water molecules organize themselves into beautiful patterns. Conversely, when placed in the presence of hateful and negative energy, the water molecules arrange themselves erratically with chaos and disharmony dominating. Consider that the human body is approximately 70% water and you will quickly realize how powerful an effect positive emotions can have on health.

Practicing gratitude is a very active state of creation. This is not something that just comes about; it takes intention to be grateful. When we focus our intention on gratitude, all negative energy falls away and we are instantly filled with powerful, loving, positive energy. Gratitude is also remarkable in its pure simplicity. All that is required is the intention to be grateful in the present moment. That's it; nothing more. Simply be thankful for what is, exactly as it is, exactly right now. What could be easier? The only thing you must do to use this handle is to look around and feel gratitude flood your heart in the present moment. You will instantly be transported to the higher vibrations of love and peace. Just like that.

You don't need to be creative about it or elaborate, complicated or sophisticated. You simply look at your present

---

[2] Masaru Emoto, translated by David A. Thayne, *The Hidden Messages in Water* (Hillsboro, OR. Beyond Words Publishing Inc., 2004).

circumstances and choose the one thing that is irritating you the most. This heightened irritation is your biggest energetic obstacle calling to you to be healed. You want to choose it and heal it instantly with gratitude. So, take the one thing that is most irritating or upsetting to you now and, in this moment, choose to feel grateful for it. The moment you find true gratitude, the irritation will be released and in its place will be unconditional love.

My husband and I have a technique for instantly shifting our energy. When one of us is irritated with the other, that person is charged with the task of finding gratitude immediately. This has never failed to instantly dissolve the dispute. The hardest part, of course, is choosing to be grateful in a moment of irritation. But once the commitment to gratitude is made, the irritation disappears.

Using gratitude is not a new technique. In fact, it is one of the most ancient secrets in humanity. All great spiritual leaders have taught the practice of gratitude in one form or another. I remember reading an article about an interview with the Dalai Lama that astounded me. When asked what the Dalai Lama thought of China, his response was simply "gratitude." Imagine how our lives could change if we replaced all negative vibrations with the positive, loving energy of gratitude. We just might find peace and happiness in the most unlikely place: within ourselves. Imagine how this shift in each of us might affect the world!

Forgiveness

After gratitude, forgiveness is the next most powerful handle to grab when we feel like we're slipping. When we hold a grudge against another person, we are emotionally bound to that person. It takes a great deal of energy to maintain a grudge. More often than not, the other person does not even realize we are holding negative energy against her or him. It's possible that the other person is not spending any energy at all. But we certainly are.

> *"To forgive is to set a prisoner free and discover the prisoner was YOU."*
>
> —Author Unknown

It is important to note that forgiveness is simply the process of releasing any anger or resentment we are holding towards another person for a perceived wrongdoing. The key word here is "perceived." Again, it all comes down to our expectations about the way things should be. Our expectations and the story we have empowered are the true cause of our discontent. Everything that is happening to us is happening perfectly and according to Universal Law. The responsibility lies with us and not with the other person. The only way to reconcile our feelings is to forgive the other person for her or his actions. By doing so, we actually forgive ourselves. This is the magic of forgiveness.

If you look into your "mirror of life" and see a perceived wrongdoing, you must remember that you need to change

on the inside before you will see a different reflection on the outside. Forgiveness gives you access to your inner world and allows you to shift who you are being. The reflection on the outside will change instantaneously. The situation will no longer have any power over you.

If you find that you are simply unable to forgive someone for something she or he has done to you, consider that you have not yet healed the wound that the person has brought to your attention. The act of forgiveness is a release, which means that you must also be willing to release the pain you are feeling as a result of the situation. There are no mistakes in the Universe, so clearly you have an emotional wound that needs your attention. It could be something that repeats itself over and over again.

The people who "cause" us to feel this pain are actually very accurate mirrors to pain we are already harbouring. These people show up in our lives to reflect this pain to us so that we will have the opportunity to heal it. The act of forgiveness gives us the ability to heal the wound and release the negativity surrounding it. An amazing paradox about forgiveness is that when we have truly forgiven a person, we actually become grateful to her or him for providing us with such an accurate reflection of what needed to be healed inside us. Forgiveness and gratitude are two of the most powerful choices we can make.

Meditation

Another incredibly powerful handle is that of inward reflection in the form of meditation. The definition of meditate is "to consider in the mind as something to be done; to intend or purpose." Put another way, meditation is an inward practice of connecting our physical bodies with our spiritual selves. The focus upon our breath serves as the conduit between the two worlds. By observing our breath, we are observing the connection between our inner spiritual world and our outer physical world. Our breath travels the distance between the two. Meditation can produce profound results.

Consider that when a group of over 4,000 people from 62 countries gathered to practice a series of Transcendental Meditations and Yogic Flying programs in the city of Washington, D.C., in July 1993, the violent crime rate dropped 21% on that day.[3] What is even more astounding is that the group predicted the crime rate drop because they had been producing similar results elsewhere. Imagine what would happen if the collective consciousness (all of us as a group) focused its intentions on love and unity instead of war and separation. There are 6 billion people on this planet, and my guess is we could effect a massive change with very little effort.

---

[3] Hagelin, et al, *Effects of Group Practice of the Transcendental Meditation Program on Preventing Violent Crime in Washington, DC: Results of the National Demonstration Project, June–July 1993* (Fairfield, Iowa: Institute of Science, Technology and Public Policy, Maharishi University of Management, 1993).

Meditation is a way for us to connect to the Universe, God, the Creator or any other name for the Divine Source, recognizing of course that we are merely an extension of this and not separate from it. By focusing inward, we dissolve the illusion that the physical world is real and we reconnect at the level of spirit. This is an excellent way to recharge our energy, in much the same way that a car refuels its energy by filling up with gas at the pump. Think of meditation as fuel for the soul. Meditation is a way for us to go to the gas pump of the Universe and fill our tanks before we begin another expedition in the physical world.

There are many different forms and practices of meditation. The most important aspect of meditation is quieting the mind in order to connect with the Divine Source of energy. There are many ways to quiet the mind. The conventional form of mediation is to sit in a quiet place and observe one's breath, as this helps to quiet the mind. Certain forms of yoga also allow for deep meditation. Yoga's focus on breath and posture creates a stillness in the mind and a connection to spirit.

Prayer is another form of meditation, as it is an intentional communion with God or the Divine Source. Prayer is most effective when the intention to create a connection to God is strong, because it is this connection to the Divine Source that creates the "energetic refill" needed to continue.

It is also possible to meditate or quiet the mind through physical movement. This is sometimes called

"active meditation" because the body is in motion. Again, the purpose is to quiet the mind and still all thoughts. If this can be achieved through the repetitive rhythm of running, walking, cycling or swimming, then so be it.

How you meditate is not as important as *whether* you meditate. You would be well served to find a meditative technique that works for you. The goal is to become aware of the connection of your spirit to the Divine Source or God or whatever you want to call it. The goal is to quiet your mind and still your thoughts so that you can be present to this divine connection and learn to draw your energy directly from the Source. Mastering this technique will greatly serve to increase your positive energy levels, which will then allow you to attract the physical manifestation of your energetic reality.

> *"We turn to God for help when our foundations are shaking, only to learn it is God who is shaking them."*
>
> — Charles C. West

Visualization

Visualization is a technique that has been used extensively in the field of competitive sports. Elite athletes are taught to visualize their desired performance with as much vivid detail as if it were really happening. The results of this technique are astounding. Studies using body monitors have shown that the same muscles fire in the same

sequence and at the same time during the visualization as in the real competition. The mind is unable to distinguish the real performance from the visualized performance. In this way, the visualization serves as a "virtual training reality" in which the athlete can perfect the skills required for peak performance.

DO THE TWIST

Try this quick and fun exercise to demonstrate an example:

- Stand with your left arm resting at your side and your right arm held straight out in front of you.
- Now, twist your torso counter-clockwise as far you can reach.
- Note how far you twist, by observing something at the edge of your periphery.
- Return to normal and rest.
- Now close your eyes and visualize yourself twisting again in the same manner, but this time twisting much further.
- Really feel yourself twisting further. Try to use all your senses to experience this twist.
- Open your eyes and repeat the same twist again.
- You will twist much further than the first time.

The tool of visualization can be used just as powerfully in manifesting your life goals. A desired performance can

be visualized in order to be perfected. This is the beginning of the BE-DO-HAVE cycle in which you visualize your "finish line" with as much vivid detail as possible as if it were really happening in the present. The important part of this process is to visualize yourself doing or achieving what you want as if it were happening right now. The energy you set in motion is composed of the positive feelings you are experiencing in your visualization. Remember, the human mind isn't able to distinguish the difference between a visualization and the real thing, so the mind instructs the body to respond with movements, hormones and feelings as if the event were occurring in real time. The Law of Attraction states that you will physically attract that which matches your energetic reality. Therefore, it will only be a matter of time before you truly experience your visualized scenario in real time.

The power of this technique will increase as you are able to engage all your senses in your visualization. You need to make the effort to provide as much detail as possible when experiencing your visualization, including the sights, smells, sounds, tastes and feelings that are present. Then, you must repeat your visualization as often as possible throughout the day to reinforce the feelings and positive energy. A great technique for shifting out of a downward spiral of self-doubt is to visualize your end contribution and the impact it will have on others' lives. Shifting the benefit and focus away from yourself and on to other

human beings is usually sufficient to shift your negative energy in the present tense back to a higher level.

Music

Several studies have shown that music has a very positive effect on the body. Specifically, classical music influences positive emotions and helps to counterbalance the effects of stress so prevalent in modern life. Dr. Charles Kimble from Dayton University has discovered that people can change a bad mood into a good one simply by listening to classical music.[4]

Music therapy is being used in the treatment of all sorts of ailments, even cancer. Music has been shown to lower blood pressure, normalize heart rates and increase the production of endorphins in the brain. All of these lead to an overall increased level of relaxation, which feels good. Remember that feeling good is the key to attracting what you really want in life. Music is a way to direct your feelings such that you can marry them with the thoughts about what it is you want in life. When you feel good, you are in alignment with the power of the Law of Attraction.

The type of music does make a difference in creating these feelings in the body. Classical music seems to be the most effective at creating strong positive emotions. The main indicator, though, is how you feel in response to

---

[4] As cited by Marcus Wynne, "Emotions in Motion," *Psychology Today* (Nov-Dec 1998): www.psychologytoday.com.

the music. If you feel uplifted and positive when listening to any beautiful music, you should keep this music available for times when you need a boost. Using music to enhance your mood is a quick way to access good feelings so you can attach them to your thoughts of what you want.

Declarations

Language is one of the most powerful tools human beings have that differentiates us from other creatures. Our spoken words can have powerful effects on our energy levels. It is very important to be mindful of our language and the energy being created as a result of the words we choose. Using negative language will usually serve to reinforce a negative energy vibration. We must choose our language to correspond with the energy level we are trying to achieve. Simply choosing to alter our language will have an instant effect on our energy levels. Consider the example of the following two sentences, both reflecting the same situation:

> *"Say what you mean and act how you feel, because those who matter don't mind, and those who mind don't matter."*
>
> —Dr. Seuss

- "This hike is killing me."
- "This hike is challenging me."

Each statement will have a profoundly different effect on the body. In the first instance, the body will respond to

the negative energy with a similar low energetic response, such that the person hiking will find that the hike continues to be a struggle. The second sentence will likely inspire the body to increase its energy level to meet the challenge of the situation. Positive language empowers and inspires a desire to improve.

Declaring our intentions in a positive way is a key step in realizing them. Another important guideline for declarations is that they must be made in the present tense. If we declare our intention in the future tense, it will always remain in the future, never coming to fruition. We must make our declarations as if they are already true and then wait for the Universe to catch up with the physical manifestation of the declarations. For example: "I have more than enough money to meet my needs" will create what we want, while "I want to have enough money to meet my needs" will always keep what we want in the future.

In the first instance we are attracting "more than enough money" and in the second instance we are actually attracting a "*want* to have enough money." In either case we will get what we attract, so we must be clear with the language of our declarations.

Exercise

Physical movement is a powerful way to shift our energy. The very act of moving causes an increase in energy as oxygen is supplied to the blood. This can be a great handle

to help halt a downward spiral because it requires no thought—only movement. When we notice that our energy is declining or we are feeling stuck, we need to get out there and move! Exercise stimulates the production of endorphins, which make us feel good, thus increasing and shifting our energy to a higher level.

Some forms of physical movement are specifically suited to changing, moving and increasing energy. The ancient practice of Tai Chi uses specific movement patterns and techniques designed to cause a desired shift in energy. When practicing Tai Chi, one can actually feel and sometimes see the energy moving throughout the body. It is impossible not to notice a shift in one's vibrational level. It might appear simple, but the results of Tai Chi are astounding. A few minutes of Tai Chi can restore positive energy to the body, providing the "refill" we need to continue our activities.

Yoga is another excellent form of physical movement because it unites the body, mind and spirit. Apart from its meditative benefits, yoga also offers great physical benefits because the postures encourage the flow of energy. Any difficulty experienced in the postures simply indicates a blockage in energy. This information or feedback is a gift we can use to work through the blockage. The body doesn't tell lies and yoga is a great way to understand where and how energy is flowing through the body.

Believe it or not, walking is one of the best forms of exercise we can practice because it involves moving most of the body in a relatively low-impact environment. All the body's organs and tissues benefit from the increase in oxygen, while at the same time we are free to experience the visual beauty of our environment. Going for a quick walk could be all you need to shift your energy upwards and get it moving again.

Finally, dancing is probably one of the most under-recognized forms of energy-enhancing exercises at our disposal. Dancing helps the body release negative energy while replacing it with positive and flowing energy. Music penetrates the body as well and infuses it with positive energetic sound vibrations. It's no wonder that

> *"Dance is the only art wherein we ourselves are the stuff in which it is made."*
> —Anonymous

children dance all the time. Their bodies are in tune with what needs to be released and this, in turn, makes room for stagnant energy to be replaced with fresher, more useful energy. All cultures have long traditions of music and dance. We would all be well served to get out there and boogie more often. Perhaps this is why aerobics took off as a form of exercise in the '80s—because it combined music, dance and aerobic activity—a perfect combination for raising energy levels.

Healthy Food

This goes right along with exercise. What you put in your body has a profound effect on your energy levels. I'm sure you've heard the adage "Garbage in, garbage out." We must be mindful of what we're putting into our bodies because the functionality of our physical bodies is what keeps us here on Earth. I don't need to tell you what happens if your body ceases to function. Just as meditation is a way to refuel the soul, food is the body's fuel. Think of the body as a high-performance automobile. When you buy a high-end car, the manufacturer insists you use only premium-grade gasoline because the engine will not function at insufficient levels of octane. This is the same for the human body. If you continuously use insufficient fuel, your performance will be adversely affected.

Numerous studies have shown that processed sugar and flour greatly reduce the performance and attention span of children in school. So why do we continue to fuel our children with packaged, processed foods and wonder why we have an epidemic of attention deficit? Our modern food supply places a great burden on our bodies to process all the modifications, pesticides and processing present. Another study has shown that the iron content in modern-day spinach has been reduced by over 90% compared with spinach from only 40 years ago. That means that even the foods that we consider to be highly nutritious have suffered from modern farming techniques and practices.

The better the fuel you put into your body, the better performance you can expect. It is much easier to transform high-quality fuel into high-quality energy. You must focus your efforts on using fuel that serves to increase and maintain your energy levels instead of fuels that provide a quick burst of energy followed by a sharp decline. Your best bet is to eat a diet that is as natural as possible with a minimal amount of processing, pesticides and modifications. Increasing the amount of organic food in your diet not only gives you a better source of nutrients, but it also encourages farming practices that reduce the burden placed on the earth.

Receiving Accolades

A natural balance exists between giving and receiving. Most of us are better at giving than we are at receiving, so we tend to shy away from really taking in the accolades and compliments being given us. This upsets the balance. In order to receive compliments from others, we must open our hearts, for that is how the energy enters the body. Our minds perceive this as a risk because, in the mind's eye, an open heart is a vulnerable one. Therefore, the tendency is to deflect the compliment back to the giver, thereby reducing the powerful energy of the compliment. When we fully open ourselves to receive an accolade, we can be overwhelmed with the high vibration of loving energy that accompanies it. This is a fabulous way to boost your energetic state.

The best way to receive a compliment is to simply reply, "Thank you." Often our tendency is to offer a compliment in return, but this only dilutes the original energy. Best is to simply stay in the moment and receive the loving energy being offered. Try it. You will feel completely different. Remember that, in receiving another's compliment, you are also giving the giver a gift by allowing a connection to be made between you.

Another similar way to boost your energy is to celebrate your accomplishments, however small they may appear. This is a very important step that often gets overlooked. Most of us are quick to criticize our every mistake but slow to realize how wonderful we really are. Since you are going to get what you focus on, it would be a good idea to focus on your greatness. As you continue to do so, you will notice that you experience yourself as greater and greater and your appreciation for yourself will grow. In turn, you will find that your appreciation for your life and others will grow as well.

Powerpods

If you want to increase and maintain your energy levels, you need to surround yourself with people whose energy you want to mirror. You can continue to support your own energy levels through the assistance of Powerpods. A Powerpod is a group of people who are committed to supporting each member of the group. These have sometimes been

called Mastermind Groups. You should be able to develop your ideas, solve your problems and celebrate your successes with the members of your Powerpod. This group is a safe place for you so that you are free to express yourself. These are the people who will cheer for you no matter how crazy your project might seem. These are people who will believe in you when you might not believe in yourself. This is a support group for your dreams.

Powerpods are easy to start. You only have to declare your desire and then begin to attract like-minded people to join your group. Groups can meet monthly, weekly, daily or randomly. They can meet in person, on a teleconference or over the internet. It doesn't really matter how you execute your Powerpod, but rather that you recognize the power in having a group of people to support you in your endeavours. The diversity of the group will allow you to see different perspectives and expand possibilities outside of your comfort zone. These are powerful ways to accelerate your growth and ideas.

Taking the "im" out of imPOSSIBLE

This technique is very powerful for shifting energy. The mind tends to divide the world into 1) things that are possible and 2) things that are impossible. If we conform to these constraints, we are limiting ourselves as to what we can achieve. If you are feeling particularly stuck, a great way to get moving is to pick something that is

imPOSSIBLE to do and then do it. Once you have achieved "the imPOSSIBLE," you are free to explore what other things might also be possible.

I developed this technique at a time in my life when I was feeling quite stuck in my own limits. I decided to randomly pick something from my imPOSSIBLE category and take on the challenge of achieving it. I chose running a marathon. As you already know, I did finish the race. This might not seem like much to most people, but believe me when I tell you that I am not a marathoner and it was probably more likely that pigs would fly. However, I took it on. I became a marathoner in the moment that I decided to do it. I filled my days with training and visualizations. The race provided me with one of those insightful, life-changing moments where things are never the same again. In an instant I finally understood what it meant to be the source of my own angst and that a shift in my own beliefs and energy was all that was needed to overcome even the most insurmountable obstacles. My ego dissolved the instant I realized that finishing that race came down to one choice I had to make about myself. In choosing to believe in myself, I was able to overcome all the physical challenges that had doomed my race minutes earlier. At the moment I crossed that finish line, I knew I had shifted my energy to a completely different level. You are reading this book because I finished that race.

Take what is imPOSSIBLE for you and do it. Then start knocking off all the other things that used to be imPOSSIBLE and aren't anymore. Once you deconstruct the division between imPOSSIBLE and POSSIBLE, you will have shifted your energy to a new level, never to return again.

Faith

Faith is the last technique for maintaining or shifting our energy levels. We must trust in the wisdom of the Universe. The definition of faith is "a belief which is not based on proof." I cannot conclusively prove to you that there is an Infinite Wisdom or God or Universal Energy,

> *"Faith is an oasis in the heart which can never be reached by the caravan of thinking."*
> —Kahlil Gibran

but I have faith that there is. It is this faith that gets me through the difficult and challenging times. I have faith that everything that is happening is perfect according to Universal Law. I have faith that the physical world is just a reflection of the spiritual world. I have faith that I have all that I need within me to alter my experience in the physical world.

They call it a "leap of faith" because at some point we must surrender the mind's need to have proof. At some point we must trust in the inner knowing that exists deep within us. At some point we must give in to the natural

> *"Sometimes your only available transportation is a leap of faith."*
> —Margaret Shepherd

order of the Universe and recognize that the only thing we can change is ourselves. At some point we must accept responsibility for our choices and reclaim the power that is already within us. The power to choose, the power to change and the power to create a reality that is absolutely perfect for us. We are not separate from God, but rather an extension of this Infinite Wisdom. Heaven is not a place to get to in the future; heaven is right here, right now. We need only see what is right in front of us.

chapter 7

THINGS THAT DON'T

*"We all cling to the past and because
we cling to the past, we become
unavailable to the present."*
—Author Unknown

As opposed to the previous chapter, this chapter outlines a few pitfalls to avoid along the path of life. The things that don't help all fall into the category of "energy-suckers." All the things described in this chapter do not support our growth and do not support maintaining high-vibration energy. We need to be aware of the effects of these energy-suckers so that we can recognize and avoid them when we encounter them. Be forewarned that if we spend any amount of our hard-earned energy thinking about these energy-suckers, we will actually empower them. It is best to steer clear of them altogether, without so much as a passing glance.

Remember that we attract what we focus on. Even if you focus on NOT wanting to indulge in any of these energy-suckers, you are still giving them your energy and they will continue to be present. If you experience any of these energy-suckers, just turn in the opposite direction or, better yet, employ one of the strategies from the previous chapter for shifting your focus.

Scarcity vs. Abundance

A mindset of scarcity creates more scarcity. Fear is the resulting emotion when the focus is on lack or scarcity. The emotion of fear vibrates at a very low level and it is very difficult to escape this vibration even with the assistance of one of the strategies in the previous chapter. Alternately, a mindset of abundance creates more abundance. It is important to remember once again that we get what we focus on, so if your starting point is a focus on scarcity then your entire experience of life will be rooted in this scarcity. There will never be enough of anything to satisfy your needs and you will never feel truly safe.

It is absolutely essential for us to break the habit of rooting our energy in the concept of scarcity. It is easy to tell if we have this problem just by listening to our language. Is the glass half-empty or half-full? We need to flip the paradigm such that we are rooting our energy in the concept of abundance. The universe is infinitely abundant and there is more than enough of everything to go around.

It might not appear that way, but remember that the way we perceive the world is simply a reflection of what is going on inside of us. If you don't believe in the infinite abundance of the universe, then that is a signal that you need to change your mindset and move out of scarcity. You know the shift has occurred when you are only able to see the universe's abundance.

SHIFT YOUR PERSPECTIVE

- Take a clean sheet of paper.
- Draw a line down the middle.
- On the left side of the line, make a list of all the things you say that come from the perspective of scarcity. (e.g., "Money doesn't grow on trees.")
- Directly opposite each saying, rewrite your wording from the perspective of abundance. (e.g., "There is more than enough money to go around.")

Negative Mainstream Media

Negativity in the media is at the top of the list of things that can literally bring down your energy in an instant. The majority of mainstream media is focused on bad news, disasters and glorified horror all designed to engage us at our lowest level. The human mind is always looking for proof that life is not a safe place, and the mainstream media gives it exactly what it is looking for. Fear is

one of the lowest-vibrating emotions and carries with it a lot of power to hold us in place. Fear has the power to immobilize us and keep us at a standstill. The mind employs the use of fear when perceiving the risk of action to be too high. Much of the mainstream media plays on this fear.

> *"Whoever controls the media, controls the mind."*
> —Jim Morrison

An enormous amount of effort is required to shift out of the negative energy generated by the mainstream media. We spend a lot of precious energy countering the effects of the horrific images, dreadful descriptions and frightful sounds that accompany most mainstream media stories. The negativity in the mainstream media is toxic to us and detrimental to our energy levels—plain and simple. The body must process this toxicity each and every time it encounters it, thus placing a huge strain on our physical systems.

News is almost invariably bad. Advertisements are always targeted at what's wrong. The majority of mainstream programming plays out at the lowest level of emotions including excessive violence, hatred and intolerance. Rarely do we encounter uplifting stories of love, unity and peace. Consider that these types of stories are called "uplifting" because they raise our energetic vibration.

In 1999 the "Media Violence Inventory: A Parent's Diary" produced by the YWCA of the U.S.A. stated that by the

end of elementary school, most children have seen 8,000 murders and 100,000 other acts of violence on TV.[5] These numbers double by age 18. It's no wonder we are now seeing dramatic increases in attention deficit, obesity and autism in our children. Our children are crying out for protection from the toxicity we are inflicting on their nascent systems. Remember Dr. Emoto's research findings on the effects of negativity on the molecular structure of water. When water samples are bombarded with negative messages, the water does not form crystals at all and displays fragmented structures and chaos. Remember, our bodies are roughly 70% water. Don't you think the mainstream media is having the same effect on our children? On us?

Another negative impact of mainstream media has to do with the Law of Attraction. As you know, the Law of Attraction states that we get what we focus on. The mainstream media focuses our attention on war, terrorism, panic and outbreaks. As a group this means that the collective consciousness is focusing on these horrible things. Guess what we will see more and more of if we continue to focus on these things? You got it—more war, terrorism, panic, outbreak.

We get what we attract. Period. If we focus on the energy of the mainstream media, we will only get more of

---

[5] A.C. Huston, et al, *Big World, Small Screen: The Role of Television in American Society* (Lincoln: University of Nebraska Press, 1992).

that energy. According to Universal Law, it can't be any other way. The only way to break the cycle is to stop giving it our attention. Mother Teresa once said that she would not participate in an anti-war rally because the focus was still on war. She said that she would only participate in a peace rally because the focus is on peace. Where is your focus? Is it on what you want or what you don't want?

I know that there will be people out there who will say, "But I have to be informed; what choice do I have?" My question in response is, "Do you really need to know how many people died in a car accident halfway across the country?" Believe me, if a news story is important enough, you will find out about it. Why subject yourself to all the anxiety that accompanies bad news? Find another information outlet or demand that your mainstream media be delivered in a different format. Believe me when I tell you that the news is brought to us by the advertisers, and the advertisers need an audience. If the news audience disappeared because the news was bad for us, then the news network would do whatever it takes to bring that audience back. The audience, not the news network, holds the power. We have to take a stand for ourselves, our children and the negative effects the mainstream media is having on all of us.

Toxins

Our environment contains numerous toxins. In and of itself, this is not disastrous, as the body is designed to

efficiently and effectively process toxins. A problem arises, however, when there is a toxic overload or a breakdown in the body's ability to process toxins. When this occurs, there is a build-up of toxicity that eventually leads to breakdown or disease. There are only two ways to avoid this: 1) maintain low levels of toxicity and/or 2) maintain the efficient performance of the body's natural abilities.

Unfortunately, we are currently experiencing a toxic overload in our culture as we continue to poison our air, our water and even our food supply. Our best bet is to avoid as many toxins as possible. Recognize, however, that it is not necessary to completely eliminate all toxins, because the body has an incredible ability to process them. You don't need to feel threatened or angry or to freak out if you are exposed to toxins. This reaction just keeps your energy focused at a low level. Rather, you need to be mindful of the toxins you are exposed to and to avoid them as much as possible. Bear in mind that a negative thought has more toxic power than any of these physical toxins.

Food

We have several very powerful choices that can keep our toxic overload from food to a minimum. Most modern farming practices are designed to maximize production levels at the minimum cost. They are not intended to maximize nutrient levels. Pesticide use, genetic modification, hormone injections, antibiotic use and non-sustainable

farming practices all lead to an increased level of toxicity in our food supply. Our best bet is to, when possible, avoid food products that were made using these methods. Choosing organic foods decreases our overall exposure to toxins, thus reducing the stress on our systems to process them. It just makes sense to ingest as few toxins as possible.

Food additives and other chemicals that are added to food place a huge burden on the body. These additives are toxic, whether or not we can find proof. They are not natural, yet they must be processed by the body. They provide little, if any, nutritional value and serve only to consume the body's energy, thereby reducing its overall effectiveness in processing everything in our systems. We must be very wary of any foods containing additives, fillers, artificial sweeteners, colouring and flavouring. These compounds add unnecessary stress to our systems, which could lead to the ultimate breakdown in the body's ability to do its job.

Drugs

Pharmaceuticals are another type of toxin that weakens the body's ability to manage its overall level of toxicity. There is, of course, a time and place for medicine—when a situation is acute or a matter of life and death. This is where Western medicine shines in its ability to provide an emergency bridge while the body repairs itself. However, in our culture, pharmaceuticals have become the mainstream approach used to mask symptoms. They do not

address the cause of the problem and often come with a host of side effects that in turn require treatment with other pharmaceuticals. The toxic burden that these drugs place on the body is enormous and requires an unusual amount of energy to eliminate.

We are better served to use pharmaceuticals in moderation and only when absolutely necessary and to otherwise seek more natural alternatives to manage our discomfort and pain. Ancient cultures managed a host of symptoms for thousands of years prior to the advent of modern medicine. Be mindful of the repercussions of taking drugs, as they are not without cost to the body. If you are conscious of the relative toll that toxins are taking on your body, you might consider an alternative in order to maintain a reasonably low level of toxins. Again, it is a matter of balance. Being mindful of your toxicity level is a very important part of maintaining a higher energy level.

Air and Water

As with our food supply, our air and water supplies are also bombarded with toxins. These days, air and water pollution are commonplace. Being mindful of how much toxicity you are exposed to is the first step in managing it. If you live in an area where there is a lot of air and water pollution, you must control your toxicity through your food intake and the reduction of pharmaceuticals. Alternatively, if you live in an area where the air and water are

clean and pure, you have a little breathing room when it comes to other toxins. Remember, your goal is to place as little a burden as possible on your body's system for eliminating toxins. The best-case scenario is clean air, clean water, organic food and no drugs.

Blame

Blame is another habit that simply does not help to keep our energy levels high. Blame is a low-vibrating emotion that keeps us down. If you find yourself laying blame, you are getting a signal that you are stuck in a low vibration. At this point you have the choice to utilize one of the techniques in the previous chapter to vault yourself out of the vibration of blame.

Laying blame keeps our focus on the external world and implies that there is something wrong "out there." This simply cannot be if we understand that the outside world is just a reflection of our inside world. Remember that it is not the mirror's fault that you are having a bad-hair day. The problem resides with your hair, not with the mirror's reflection of your hair. Blaming others is a futile waste of time and energy. However, blame can serve as a useful signal that your focus is on the reflection rather than on the real

> *"What is, is. What isn't, isn't. You become so obsessed with what isn't that you miss what is."*
>
> —Author Unknown

picture. When you notice that you have moved into blame, you are also able to understand that a simple shift to your inside world is all it will take to alter your outside world. If you handle the complaint for which you are blaming someone else, you will see it miraculously disappear without the other person so much as lifting a finger. Living is an inside-out process. You must look to your outside world for feedback about how you are progressing on the inside.

Negative People

The Law of Allowing states that we must allow what is happening to happen. There will always be people who do not believe in what you are doing. If you recognize them as simply the reflection of that part of yourself that has doubts about what you are doing, then you are free from their negativity. The problem is that if you indulge in believing their negativity, you will find yourself locked in a low vibration of energy.

We attract what we focus on. If you find yourself encountering negative people, you must understand that you were responsible for putting out negative energy in the first place. That is the only way you could have attracted such negativity. Recognizing that you are actually the source of this negativity provides you the opportunity to go inward to change your energy. You will then find that changing your energy immediately eliminates your negative experience

on the outside. Focusing on the negativity will only serve to bring you more of the same negative energy.

Negative Self-Talk

Empowering that little voice in our heads that reinforces our negative beliefs is another habit that keeps us down. This is one of the most powerful sources of toxicity. We must do whatever it takes to break out of these self-defeating habits! Sometimes breaking a habit can be as simple as shouting, "NO THANK YOU!" when we notice the negativity rising to the surface. The purpose of doing this is to interrupt the pattern of negative self-talk. Once the pattern is interrupted, we can choose to replace it with something more positive and uplifting. Everyone suffers from some degree of self-doubt. The problem arises when we give these thoughts our energy, even if we are trying to focus on not having them. We will get more of what we focus on. The best way to deal with this is to simply choose to remain in a state of gratitude for all our wonderful and redeeming qualities.

Empowering Fears

Fear is a natural emotion created by the mind in an effort to keep us safe. Everyone has fears. Acknowledging our fears and being controlled by our fears are two totally different things. When we acknowledge our fear, it means

we are allowing the energy to pass through as we experience the events of life. When we are controlled by our fear, it means we focus our attention on the fear and the story about the fear, thus empowering the fear energy to control our actions. The mind uses fear as a tool to keep us in our safety zone. The problem is that fear is one of the lowest-vibrating emotions, so we are only going to attract other low vibrations when in a state of fear. This will prevent us from attracting anything in the realm of love, peace or happiness. Allowing your fear to prevail stands in the way of your receiving that which you said you wanted and asked for from the Universe.

However, fear can also be a gift because it indicates exactly which parts of us need to be healed in order to remove any blockages in energy. It is important, therefore, not to ignore our fears but rather to learn to use them to help us get what we want. Fear is just a signal from the mind that

"Fear is an acronym for: False Evidence Appearing Real"
—Author Unknown

danger is present. We can use our fear to understand exactly what our minds perceive as dangerous and to determine in the moment if this is true. Usually most fears are created in childhood and no longer serve us in adulthood. Recognizing a recurring fear as feedback from the Universe as to the location of an energy block is a huge

step towards being free of fear. Allowing your fear to direct your actions is a sure-fire way to keep yourself rooted in a cycle of low-vibration energy.

Being Attached to an Outcome

The attachment to results looking a certain way is another thing that keeps us in a low-vibration energy state. In an effort to maintain a grip on reality, our minds make up stories about how situations "should" be. This allows our minds a context for feeling safe and secure. As long as the events unfold according to our minds' plans, everything is okay. If, however, the events should stray from this story, then all havoc may be wreaked in our minds. This havoc is then transferred to the body in the form of low-vibrating emotions such as fear, anxiety and worry. As long as you remain attached to your version of how things "should" be, you will continue to be trapped in the levels of fear, anxiety or worry.

"If you think your whole life is going wrong just because so much of it is going wrong, then you're wrong. Mostly when things go wrong, they're meant to go wrong, so we can outgrow what we have to outgrow."

—Author Unknown

It is very important to remain grounded in the Law of Allowing. This gives us the power we need to free ourselves from our attachment. If we focus

on allowing events to unfold exactly as they are, we release ourselves from the burden of the negative emotions. This is challenging for the control freak in us who believes we must control our external circumstances in order to be safe and secure. Anytime is a good time to practice faith in the Universe and to understand that the Universe doesn't make mistakes. Remember, it's all good.

Constant Review

The tendency to need proof is not an easy one to overcome. Humans have a very deep-seated desire to see something first and then believe it. But the Universe actually operates exactly opposite to that desire—first we must believe it and then we will see it. This is the Law of Attraction. One way to sabotage your efforts is to constantly review your physical reality, searching for proof that the Law of Attraction is working. Remember that there is always a lag as the Universe strives to match our physical reality to our energetic reality. We send a lot of mixed signals that take time to play out. Constantly looking for proof that the Law of Attraction is, in fact, not working will only send more energy in the direction of "not getting." Constant review is just another form of focusing on what's "not there" and will only get you more of that. Resist the tendency to require proof that it works. It does.

Trusting and having faith in the Universe is the best cure for our need to see proof. If you can let go of the need

to know and just allow the events to unfold according to the infinite wisdom of the Universe, you will find that life flows with a lot more ease. Constant review and criticism of your results keeps your energy focused at the level of doubt, which is a low-vibrating emotion. This will prevent you from shifting into the higher vibrations required to attract the things you really want. You must be mindful of your focus and steer clear of the need to find proof.

Giving Up

Quitting is a guaranteed strategy for not getting what you want. Quitting is the direct result of empowering our doubts in our own abilities as well as in the Universe. Quitting is the result of maintaining our energy at a low vibration. When we give up on a dream, we are essentially sending the signal to the Universe that we don't really want what we said we wanted. The Universe obliges by ensuring that we do not receive it. Remember the genie's words: "Your wish is my command." The Law of Attraction works to give us what we focus on, whether we are asking to get something or NOT to get something. Either way, the Universe replies, "Your wish is my command."

Most people give up at the most critical time in the pursuit. Usually it is at a time when holding on for just a little longer would produce the desired result. The quitting usually occurs at the very opportunistic point of maximum growth and change. This time is usually preceded by a

level of discomfort that is signalling the occurrence of a great change. This time is usually accompanied by unpleasant emotions, and the fear of merely experiencing these emotions can often be enough to cause a retreat. We sometimes don't realize that if we would just allow these emotions to pass and release the energy associated with them, we could finally be free to receive that which we are seeking. This requires a leap of faith. If you find yourself in a cycle of giving up, this is a signal to watch for the point of retreat. At that point, you can consciously maintain a high level of energy so as to break through the threshold from which you have habitually retreated. As Winston Churchill once said, "Never, never, never, never give up."

Focusing on Obstacles

It is well known in the world of downhill skiing that the fastest way to ski down a mountain covered in moguls is to find the straightest path through the field of moguls and focus on staying on that path. If you focus on the size and number of the moguls, you'll be dead meat. It is the same in real life. We get what we focus on. If our focus is on obstacles, we will see obstacles at every turn. If our focus is on solutions, we will easily be able to handle and solve any problems that come our way.

There is a huge difference between problem-focused thinking and solution-focused thinking. When we focus on problems, we send a signal to the Universe that we

want more problems. You can see how this is not a good thing. Focusing on solutions sends a signal to the Universe that we want more solutions, and the Universe is obliged to deliver. If you want to keep your energy levels high, you must be very mindful of which mindset you are empowering.

Staying Stuck

Everyone gets stuck in some form of energy blockage from time to time. This is normal. Getting stuck is not a problem; *staying* stuck is. Remember Newton's Third Law of Thermodynamics—an object at rest tends to stay at rest unless acted upon by an outside force. It takes a huge force to stop our momentum, but it also takes a huge force to get unstuck. If you can only keep moving, even just a little, you will find it easier to regain your speed. If you get stopped, you will need to expend a great deal more energy just to get moving in the right direction

> *"It does not matter how slowly you go, so long as you do not stop."*
> —Confucius

again. The longer you stay stuck, the more stuck you become and the more force you will need to get moving again. It is in your best interest to avoid staying stuck.

You can do this in a number of ways. Diverting your attention is usually one of the most effective ways to avoid staying stuck. By doing so, you shift your energy away from

the problem. Then, when your focus returns to the situation, you may have renewed energy and a little more perspective on how to keep moving. Another way to avoid staying stuck is to keep moving no matter what happens. This means that taking even the smallest of baby steps towards your goal is better than getting and staying stuck. You must find *something* you can accomplish and then do it. Once you finish it, you need to celebrate your success. This way you refocus your energy on what you are doing well instead of on what you are doing wrong. If you do this enough times, you will find that you have built enough momentum to get moving again.

> *"Keep your face to the sunshine and you will not see the shadows."*
> —Helen Keller

The bottom line is that you will always be presented the opportunity to choose between an action that supports your higher purpose and one that does not. At the end of the day, the responsibility to choose rests solely with you. The life you experience is a direct result of the choices you make about how to maintain your energy level. The only thing you can do if you are not satisfied with your physical experience is to turn inward and shift your energy.

"No pressure, no diamonds."

—Mary Case

chapter 8

THE LIFE OF *YOUR* DREAMS

*"Since everything in life is but an experience
perfect in being what it is, having nothing to do
with good or bad, acceptance or rejection,
one may well burst out in laughter."*

—Long Chen Pa

It is your birthright to live the life of your dreams. You were not put on this earth to live anyone else's version of life—only your own. It is your responsibility to determine what your desired version of life is and then pursue this with reckless abandon. Life is meant to be enjoyed, experienced and savoured. Some people may try to convince you otherwise, but you don't have to empower them. Why not empower, instead, the fundamental belief that life can be a game—a fun game at that? Once you understand the Universal Laws, you are free to master the game of life. You are free to experiment with what pleases you and what does not. When you are able to reframe

everything in your life as working out "perfectly," exactly according to the rules of the game, you can finally be free to "play around with the pieces" until you produce the outcome you truly want.

LIFE IS NOT A COMPLICATED MESS. IN FACT, LIFE IS QUITE SIMPLE. IT ALL BOILS DOWN TO THIS PROCESS FOR ALL OF US:

1. We <u>want</u> IT ("IT" can be anything).
2. We <u>do</u> some things.
3. We either <u>get IT or get FEEDBACK.</u>
4. Repeat (using the feedback).

That's pretty much life in a nutshell. For some reason, human beings like to complicate matters and inject drama wherever possible. The simple process of life gets all muddied up and starts to look a little like this:

1. We *want* "IT," but deep down we really don't think we deserve it, so we never tell anyone that we want it. If we should happen to tell someone that we want it, she or he might tell us that it is impossible and so we may never even try to get it. If we do try to get it, we get frustrated at the first sign that it isn't working out. We might just settle for something "more sensible" so as to avoid the whole thing.
2. We *do* some actions but aren't really going after the thing we *really* want, so we do these actions half-heartedly and without much enthusiasm. The actions are not fun

because they are not inspired by our true desires. If we do happen to go after something we really want, often our actions don't make sense because we don't have a clear picture of our finish line and our minds are constantly trying to sabotage our efforts in order to keep us safe. We indulge all of our minds' stories as if they were "absolute truth" and so we don't really believe we can get what we want. In the end, we settle for something "sensible" with a lot less risk but a guaranteed payout.

3. We either *get IT or get FEEDBACK.* Either way our minds make up a story about the outcome, and again we engage it as the "absolute truth." If we were not successful in getting what we wanted, our minds usually use it as proof that we weren't good enough or deserving enough or that we were bad or wrong in some way. We hardly ever pay attention to the valuable feedback we just received. If we do get what we wanted, we don't really celebrate it because deep down we still don't think we deserve it or we use our success to prove to others that we are somehow better than they are. Either way, we still don't feel good about it. We blame our circumstances for how we feel and set our sights on something else that we can pin all our happiness on.

4. Repeat. In this case, we don't actually change who we are being using the feedback from our outcome. We just go back and try to do the same thing again, hoping for a different result. We continue this cycle over and

over again until we feel we're going nuts. Then we give up and go after something else.

Sound familiar? It doesn't have to be this hard or monotonous. Life is simple. Life is fun. It's all good, even the "bad" things. There are no accidents in the Universe, ever! Let's review the entire game right here, right now. Here is a simple, empowering way to play the *game of life*. Use it if it works for you:

Rules

1. The Law of Attraction.
2. The Law of Deliberate Creation.
3. The Law of Allowing.

Purpose of the Game

To live the best and fullest life possible while here on Earth.

Assumptions about Self and Life

1. We are a part of (not separate from) *the Infinite Universe* [insert your name for it here (e.g., "God")].
2. We are loved.
3. Anything is possible.
4. Life is a mirror.

How the Game Is Played

1. *Want* IT ("IT" can be anything).
2. *Do* some things.

3. Either *get IT or get FEEDBACK.*

4. Repeat (using the feedback).

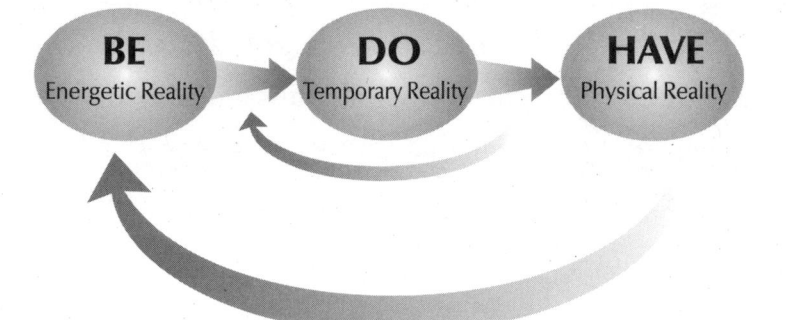

The Feedback Loop of Life

Obstacles

1. When met with an obstacle, deal with it directly. Running in the opposite direction will adversely affect forward progress.

2. Obstacles will repeat themselves until they are adequately dealt with.

3. We can only move to the next level of the game when we have effectively dealt with all the obstacles at our current level.

How to Win the Game

1. Play 100%, expect 0%.

2. Win by enjoying playing the game itself.

Any drama or story that gets added to the game is done so by the mind and is not a real part of the game. These

stories will slow down our progress and ultimately hinder our enjoyment of the game. If we focus on the other players in the game, we will also find our progress slowing and our enjoyment decreasing. It is usually best to keep our focus on ourselves and our surroundings because all the answers are right in front of us and the ability to change the outcome rests inside of us.

Destiny

You may have heard someone say, "It just wasn't meant to be." This is true to the extent that the Law of Attraction always works and delivers exactly according to our energy, despite what our minds might want. However, destiny is not something that is pre-determined before we are born and that we therefore have no impact on. What we call "destiny" is simply a way of justifying our disappointment.

"I think of life itself now as a wonderful play that I've written for myself ... and so my purpose is to have the utmost fun playing my part."
—Shirley MacLaine

Let's look at an example, again focussing on the area of career. Let's say you really want to get a certain fabulous job. You create the desire and you create a plan and start taking all sorts of inspired action. Then you find out that you did NOT get the job. You are very disappointed, but you dismiss the

outcome with "It wasn't meant to be" and chalk it up to "destiny." The problem here is that you missed the opportunity to use the feedback you got. The outcome is telling you that there was a disconnect between your starting point and your finish line. Somewhere between the creation of the intention and the outcome of the physical reality, mixed signals were sent. Given that our physical reality will always match our energetic reality, we can understand in this example that at the level of energetic reality you were not clear. This is awesome feedback. All you have to do now is go back to where you create your energetic reality and work out a few of the bugs. That's all that stands between you and your fabulous job. OR, you can just give up and chalk it up to destiny while you keep plugging away at the job you hate.

Another commonly held belief about destiny is that there is some grand plan for each of us that is determined by a higher power and completely removed from us. In this scenario, we plug along in life accepting our "fate" as truth and as something we have no influence over. Each and every disappointment is dismissed as "not part of my path," so that instead of learning and growing through our failures we just perpetuate our misery. There may be some truth to the notion that we have come to this earth to learn specific lessons for our spiritual growth. However, we have our own free will to determine if, how and when we will learn these lessons.

Life is not preordained, running out its course while we suffer the inevitable. We are creating our lives every single day, every single minute. In each moment we have the creative power to completely alter the outcome. We have the creative power to attract absolutely anything we want. We are part of the Infinite Creation and are subject to the Laws of the Universe. Anything we want is absolutely within our reach.

If you are NOT getting what you want, you are creating some type of block to ensure you do not receive it. If you are NOT getting what you want, you need to take a moment to consider the feedback and then USE IT to your advantage. You must search out the blocks, deal with them and then open up the pathways to the life of your dreams.

Luck

Luck is another misunderstood and often misused word. Luck is not random. Luck is used to describe "being in the right place at the right time." But if we understand the Laws of the Universe, we realize that we created and attracted that moment in time, so it really wasn't "luck" but rather the manifestation of deliberate creation. Luck is an arbitrary way of explaining why some people get good things in life and others do not. The concept of luck as a random occurrence is impossible, according to the Universal Laws. The Law of Attraction states that we get

what we attract. End of story. Therefore, if you got "lucky" and won the lottery, at some level you attracted it. If you got "unlucky" and got mugged, at some level your energetic vibration was matched with that of the mugger. The Universe is not random; it is very, very efficient. There is no such thing as luck. Absolutely everything that happens is governed by Universal Law. Everything!

Spiritual Lessons

Each person has a different set of spiritual lessons to learn that can only be learned via a physical experience. We are here now to learn these lessons. The lives we create are done so by us to perfectly facilitate these lessons. We are constantly receiving feedback from the Universe as to where to look and what to do next. We need to become conscious of these signals and start using them to our advantage. We might as well enjoy ourselves while we are here, so it is best to create a physical reality that pleases us.

Recognize, though, that when this physical reality is unpleasant, we have created that too. That is where our lessons lie. We must look to our failures for feedback as to what is standing in

"Whatever a person's mind dwells on intensely and with firm resolve, that is exactly what he [she] becomes."

—Shankaracharya

> *"You are never asked to do more than you are able without being given the Strength and Ability to do it."*
>
> —Eileen Caddy

our way. Our lessons are contained in our obstacles. We will be able to learn our lessons easily once we are able to clearly see the obstacle. When the obstacle is exposed, we will inherently know what has to be done to clear the obstacle from our path. Once the obstacle has been removed, we will be free to move on to the next lesson. This process will continue until we have accomplished everything we came here to learn. At that point, we will leave this physical existence.

Miracles and Magic

Consider for a moment that there are things we simply do not understand about this world. Just be open to that possibility. How do you explain the inexplicable? Should you accept it, ignore it or dismiss it? What if you could allow for it? What would be possible for you if the "impossible" were completely possible? What career might you have? What relationships would you enjoy? What disease could you cure?

There have been countless documented cases of utterly inexplicable things happening since the beginning of time. These mysteries provide insight into the awesome power of the Universe and shed light on the vast array of information

that is simply not understood. Did Jesus really walk on water? Did Norman Cousins really save his own life simply by laughing? Did that blind man teach himself to see? Can people really levitate? Does a psychic really read minds? Is there such a thing as a fairy? Can children really see angels? What if all of it really happened? What does that mean for everything we consider impossible?

If you can believe in miracles and magic, you might be able to see that anything is possible. Remember that faith is about believing in something without having any proof. You will also recall that the mind cannot tell the difference between the visualization of something and its physical occurrence. If you can visualize something that once seemed impossible and then have faith that everything is possible, you'll see how it is quite conceivable that that thing just might come about. That's all it takes, and it starts with the belief. Physical reality will always align with energetic reality. Always.

Living Your Own Life

The rest of this chapter is dedicated to helping you reach for *your* stars and create a life that you absolutely love, using the techniques outlined in this book. This is not the place to play small and accept "sensible" options. This is your chance

> *"For those who believe, no proof is necessary. For those who don't believe, no proof is possible."*
>
> —Author Unknown

to play big and to reclaim your enthusiasm for life. What would you attempt if you *knew* your success was guaranteed? What would you do if you knew you only had one year left to live? Life is meant to be lived vigorously.

I believe that everyone has a unique purpose and a distinct gift to give the rest of the world. I also believe that each one of us creates the perfect scenario in which to deliver this gift, all the while learning the lessons that need to be learned. Your commitment to your higher purpose is what will give you the strength to continue when confronted with challenges and obstacles. Your vision for contributing to others is what will give you energy when you get stopped and stuck in your own story. Being clear about your purpose and the contribution you can make to others is integral in getting the most out of life. Your vision must be YOUR vision. It must come from deep inside you.

> *"There are only two ways to live your life. One is as though nothing is a miracle. The other is as though everything is a miracle."*
> —Albert Einstein

Have you ever seen those little plastic puzzles where the pieces all move around to create a big picture? I use these puzzles in my workshops and speeches to illustrate that though each of us is unique, we are all part of the same big picture. When the pieces are in their correct location, the picture works. However, when even just one piece is out of

place, the picture doesn't work and there is chaos in the puzzle. It is the same thing in real life. Each of us must find our place in the big picture. You must find your place. There isn't a better or more important place. There is only *your* place. There is only *your* path. There is only right now.

42-Day Projects

Forty-two-day projects are an excellent way to play the game of life. They are long enough to allow us to accomplish something, but short enough to maintain our attention. The number 42 also holds great significance. Someone once taught me that it takes the human body an average of about 42 days to replace its cells (obviously some take a lot longer and some a lot less). This means that we are essentially a new person approximately every 42 days. Another significant fact about 42 is that it takes 21 days to create a habit and 42 days to master it. Also, according to *The Hitchhiker's Guide to the Galaxy*,[6] the answer to "life, the universe and everything" is "42." There is something serendipitous about the number 42, so I created the "42-day project." This technique gives us a chance to observe the Feedback Loop of Life and create a life we love.

THERE ARE FOUR STEPS TO THE 42-DAY PROJECT:

1. BE
2. DO
3. HAVE
4. REPEAT for 42 days

---

[6] Douglas Adams, *The Hitchhiker's Guide to the Galaxy* (England: Pan Books, 1979), 152.

BE

What do you want to have? This step is where you choose to be the deliberate creator you are and declare to the Universe what you want. Then you have to BE that outcome by transporting yourself to the "energetic reality" and BEING in the energy. You must describe this energetic reality in as much detail as possible, in the present tense, as if you are really experiencing it. Remember that this is where the attraction energy gets sent out into the Universe to attract that which you want. You will know you are complete with this step when you have a clear picture of your finish line. This will also help you recognize it when you get there.

DO

Once you have a clear picture of your finish line, you need to fill your time with inspired action. The "doing" phase is a "temporary reality" whereby the Universe is hastily arranging things such that your physical reality matches the energetic reality you just finished creating. During this "temporary reality," there is an opportunity to create an inspired action plan. It is important that this plan starts with the end in mind (i.e., our finish line). You can then begin to break down your finish line into generations of goal babies until you have a manageable list of things to do on a daily basis. As you go about doing these inspired actions, you must pay close attention to the signals you get from the Universe as to whether or not you are on the most straightforward path to

your finish line. You can make minor adjustments during the temporary reality according to these signals.

HAVE

There will come a point in time where you will either get what you want or get feedback. If you get what you want, then you need to be sure to celebrate your success and enjoy the fruits of your labour. If you get feedback instead of getting what you want, you need to take the time to understand the feedback and learn from it. Here, observe what it is that you did get. Then look for the signs as to where the blockage occurred that prevented your attracting what you really wanted. Deal with the obstacle if possible.

REPEAT

If you got feedback instead of what you wanted, then this would be the right time to adjust your energy and give it another try. You need to use the information contained in your failure to help you readjust your creation and attraction. You must try another technique to raise or change your energy. You must BE something different. This will ensure a different result. Whatever you get, you must continue to repeat the process for 42 days.

How You Do Anything

Forty-two-day projects are an excellent way to test the procedures in this book without investing a lot of time. You can

find out what works for you and what doesn't. You can also determine what patterns exist in your own life, because they will show up within the context of the 42-day project. T. Harv Eker once said, "How you do anything is how you do everything." The 42-day project is a microcosm of your life. It is a way to observe on a smaller scale how the bigger aspects of your life work. I can guarantee that if something surfaces during a 42-day project, it has also surfaced in your life previously. Resolving it in the context of the 42 day project will also eliminate it from the bigger picture of your life.

The other great thing about 42-day projects is that you can have a bunch of them running at once. It is usually best to stagger their start dates so you are not in the same phase of each project at the same time. Consequently, when you are challenged or stuck in the process for one project, you can focus on a different one. This refocusing usually allows a new solution to surface in the other project because you have taken the pressure off. Plus, having multiple 42-day projects means that you will be producing outcomes all the time, thus increasing the sheer fun of living.

42 IDEAS

- Grab a clean sheet of paper.
- List 42 different ideas for creating a 42-day project.
- Choose one and start it tomorrow.

A Vision for Humanity

If anything were possible, what would you wish for? Imagine a world in which each person is living completely aligned with her or his true self and higher purpose in harmony with every other creature on the planet. Close your eyes and just imagine it. This is what I am envisioning every chance I get. Believe it or not, it actually starts with me living completely aligned to my higher purpose and in harmony with every other creature on Earth. Once I have mastered this "energetic reality" within myself, I will come to see it in the physical world. Until that time, I will continue to use the feedback I get from the Universe and deal with my obstacles as they appear. What gets me out of bed in the morning is my commitment to "reflect the light that is in each and every person." I believe that every single one of us has a light inside. My purpose is to be the mirror for everyone's light and reflect it back so that they too can see it.

I have always been moved to tears by the following passage from *A Return to Love* by Marianne Williamson. It is so good that Nelson Mandela decided to use it within his 1994 inaugural speech when he was given the trust and confidence to rebuild the nation of South Africa. I use this powerful passage in my workshops. You can also download a beautifully formatted version of it from my website www.GinaML.com.

"Our deepest fear is not that we are inadequate.
Our deepest fear is that we are powerful beyond measure.
It is our light, not our darkness, that most frightens us.
We ask ourselves, 'Who am I to be brilliant,
gorgeous, talented, and fabulous?'
Actually, who are you not to be?
Your playing small doesn't serve the world.
There is nothing enlightened about shrinking so that
others won't feel insecure around you.
We were born to make manifest the glory that is within us.
It's not just in us, it's in everyone.
As we let our own light shine, we unconsciously
give others permission to do the same.
As we are liberated from fear, our presence
automatically liberates others."

—Marianne Williamson

A Challenge

We are here to make manifest the glory that is within us. We are here to make a difference in this world. If you are wondering if this is the time that you should be doing something, all you need to do is look around. You are alive now, so now is the time. Every single person has a unique gift to give to humanity, and humanity is begging for those gifts. Everywhere we turn, people are in need. They are pleading for our gifts.

It can be frightening to let our lights shine. It can be terrifying to expose our true selves for everyone to see. Vulnerability is not the mind's favourite place. But you will suffer if you continue to suppress your true self and higher purpose. Your spirit will suffer from lack of expression. Your soul will suffer from lack of freedom. This in and of itself is a tragedy. But this is not the worst tragedy.

People everywhere will suffer if you continue to suppress your true self and higher purpose. People everywhere will suffer if you keep your spirit hidden and your soul locked up. It's not just about *you*; it's about this whole world. You will never ever realize the impact you can have unless you make it. No one ever reveres what doesn't get done. Humanity is always grateful for what does get done.

> *"If you deliberately plan on being less than you are capable of being, then I warn you that you'll be unhappy for the rest of your life."*
>
> —Abraham Maslow

If not now, when?

If not you, who?

As Jean Houston once said at a conference I attended, "This is the time. You are the people."

"If you want to SEE it, then first you have to BE it."
—Gina Mollicone-Long

chapter 9

THE 42 THINGS THAT WILL POSITIVELY CHANGE YOUR LIFE

"We either make ourselves miserable, or we make ourselves strong. The amount of work is the same."
—Carlos Castaneda

1. **KEEP A JOURNAL.**
    Make sure you write in it. You never know when the insight from a previous day will come in handy. Record your feelings as well as your thoughts. Buy journals that inspire you instead of the plain black ones with lined pages. Try to write every day at around the same time. Include a section on gratitude. Read your old journals.

2. **CELEBRATE ONE SUCCESS EVERY SINGLE DAY.**
    Do not let yourself fall asleep without celebrating something you accomplished that day. Even if you can only produce freshly cleaned teeth, give it your best hoot-and-holler. It is important to be enthusiastic when celebrating your successes. You cannot overdo this enthusiasm. The more, the better.

3. **MAKE A LIST OF 100 THINGS YOU WANT TO DO BEFORE YOU DIE.**

    Start doing them tomorrow. Check them off as you accomplish them. Try to do one thing on your list every year on your birthday. Review the list at least once a year and add to it as necessary. Record your adventures in your journal. Take a picture of yourself doing each thing.

4. **READ INSPIRING QUOTES.**

    Read at least one insight every day. Subscribe to a service that delivers a quote to your inbox every day. Recognize the wisdom in the quote you receive on any given day. Try to understand this wisdom and apply it throughout your day. Write your own quotes. Publish them.

5. **SURROUND YOURSELF WITH COLOUR.**

    Every colour has its own vibration. Pick a colour-of-the-day. Try to wear it, eat it, drink it and notice it everywhere. Write with coloured ink and on coloured paper. Dream in colour.

6. **GIVE AT LEAST ONE HUG EVERY SINGLE DAY.**

    Make sure you hug heart-to-heart so that your heart is touching the heart of the other person. Be firm with your hug—no wishy-washy hugs allowed. Try giving hugs instead of shaking hands with the new people you meet.

7. **SAY "I LOVE YOU" TO THE IMAGE IN YOUR MIRROR EVERY MORNING.**

You can also include "good morning" and "you're beautiful." This is an excellent way to start your day and to remind yourself that you are responsible for loving yourself.

8. **SAY "I LOVE YOU" TO SOMEONE ELSE EVERY SINGLE DAY.**

Try to pick a different person every day. Be sincere. Look them in the eye. Feel your heart reaching out to theirs. Say it to people who least expect it.

9. **PERFORM RANDOM, ANONYMOUS ACTS OF KINDNESS.**

Try to do something kind for someone every day. Make sure they do not know it was you. Take pleasure in the fact that they are trying to figure out who did it. If someone finds you out, encourage them to pay it forward to performing another act of kindness for someone else.

10. **PICK UP EVERY SINGLE PENNY YOU FIND AND BLESS IT.**

Consider it a gift when you find money on the ground. Demonstrate to the Universe that you are ready to accept any and all money that it wants to throw your way. Put that money towards your financial freedom.

11. MAKE A LIST OF EVERYTHING YOU ARE GRATEFUL FOR AND CARRY IT WITH YOU.

Update the list as often as you can, especially when you are feeling down. Read the list every time you need to boost your energy. Record the list in your voice and listen to it while you work out or drive your car.

12. TALK TO STRANGERS.

Remember that you have attracted every single person into your life based on what you want. Find out why they are in your life. Ask questions. Listen for the answers. See the light in each and every person you meet.

13. SING OUT LOUD EVERY DAY.

Do it in the shower or in the car. Test the range of your vocal chords. Imitate your favourite performers. Play air guitar or air drums. Do it with enthusiasm. Always sing to your children. Always sing with your children. Always sing the national anthem.

14. DANCE EVERY SINGLE DAY.

Do it while you are getting dressed or whenever you hear a catchy beat. Tap your toes whenever you can. Wiggle your hips. Always dance with your children. Take your spouse for a twirl when you get home from work. Always dance at weddings.

15. TALK TO YOUR HOUSEPLANTS.

Do this every day. Tell them your plan for the day. Tell them what you are grateful for. Tell them that you appreciate the fine job they are doing enhancing your home by providing it with nourishing oxygen. Ask them to keep an eye on your place. Feed them the same water you drink.

16. MEDITATE EVERY DAY.

Find a meditation technique that works for you and practice it. Give yourself some time to quiet your mind. Think of this as pulling up to the Universal gas pump to refuel your soul. Focus your meditation on love and peace.

17. LISTEN TO BEAUTIFUL MUSIC.

Explore different types of music and how they make you feel. Stick with the ones that give you warm fuzzies. Remember that people like Mozart and Beethoven are considered geniuses for a reason.

18. DO ONE THING EVERY DAY THAT SCARES YOU.

It can be anything, even talking to someone you don't know. Be sure to look for the opportunity to do something scary. Remember, scary for you does not mean scary for someone else. You will know when you are scared. Recognize it, acknowledge it and then do it anyway.

19. PLAY AT 100% AND EXPECT 0%.

Give your full effort every single time you do something. Never hold back, especially your enthusiasm. If you don't expect anything in return, you'll never be disappointed.

20. TRAIN YOURSELF TO ENJOY SOMETHING YOU DON'T CURRENTLY LIKE.

My husband taught me this trick. Think of it as a game. You can really expand your comfort zone with this one. So far, he has learned to like such things as olives, black coffee and scotch whiskey.

21. REMEMBER OTHER PEOPLE'S BIRTHDAYS.

Most people crave acknowledgement and attention. Show other people that you notice them by remembering their birthday. Use your computer software to remind you when their special day arrives. Send an email, an e-card or make a phone call. It makes a world of difference.

22. REMEMBER OTHER PEOPLE'S NAMES.

Do whatever it takes to remember someone's name when you meet them. Devise a system and use it. Test yourself. Commit yourself to remembering their name. This forces you to be fully present in the moment.

23. CREATE AT LEAST ONE POWERPOD.

Create a list of people. Set a time. Have a meeting. Use your Powerpod to expand your ideas and create big things. Ask for help from your Powerpod instead of trying to solve everything yourself.

24. TAKE THE "IM" OUT OF IMPOSSIBLE AT LEAST ONCE A YEAR.

Make a list of things that are imPOSSIBLE for you. Put the list on your bulletin board. Choose one thing each year to knock off your list and watch as your realm of POSSIBILITY grows.

25. LAUGH EVERY SINGLE DAY.

Laughter really is the best medicine. Watch funny movies. Get a joke-of-the-day book or calendar. Tell jokes. Read funny books and comics. Listen to people's funny stories. Laughter oxygenates your blood and floods your system with endorphins.

26. CONSTANTLY REMIND YOUR CHILDREN THAT YOU BELIEVE IN THEM.

Make it a point to tell your children every single day that "they can do it"—no matter how small their task may appear. Reflect to them this belief so that they will begin to identify it as their own.

27. STAND UP FOR WHAT YOU BELIEVE IN.

Know what is important to you. State your beliefs firmly, avoiding confrontation. Disregard the need to please everyone and remain focused in your integrity. Taking a stand allows others the courage to do the same.

28. ACCEPT YOUR PARENTS FOR WHO THEY ARE.

Your parents did the best they could with what they had. You will come to understand this if you have your own children. Recognize that there are no accidents in the Universe and your parents are exactly what you needed for your life lessons.

29. SPREAD JOY AND HAPPINESS.

Be the example of what you want to see in the world. Focus on joy and happiness. Refuse to be cynical. Be the uplifting light in everyone's day. Believe in the possibility of magic and miracles.

30. TALK TO YOURSELF.

Be kind. Be loving. Talk often and with enthusiasm. Ask yourself hard questions. Challenge yourself to grow. Tell jokes to yourself. Read out loud to yourself.

31. STAND NEAR THE OCEAN WHENEVER YOU HAVE THE CHANCE.

The ocean air is charged with negative ions that attach themselves to free radicals. Think of it as a Velcro filter for your negative energy. It is a fantastic way to clean your aura.

32. EAT REAL FOOD.

Eat fruit. Eat vegetables. Buy meat from a butcher who sings while he works. Buy full-fat peanut butter and sour cream. If you are going to drink soda pop, drink the real thing and avoid the artificial sweeteners. Don't bother with low-fat cookies. If you are going to indulge, eat the real thing.

33. BUY A SANDWICH FOR A HOMELESS PERSON.

Ask them what they'd like to have. Get them a gourmet extra special sandwich from a fancy shop. Better yet, take them to a restaurant and spend some time talking with them.

34. BABY-SIT FOR A SINGLE PARENT.

Make an offer to give a single parent a break and baby-sit for free. Most single parents are struggling to make ends meet and also have very little time for themselves. You can also offer to take their kids out so they can enjoy a little peace and quiet in their own home.

35. THINK ABOUT WORLD PEACE EVERY SINGLE DAY.

Meditate about it. Pray about it. Visualize it. Believe it. World peace will only come about when the collective consciousness can envision it. Focus on peace. Be peaceful.

36. BLESS YOUR ENEMIES AND YOUR CHALLENGES.

Remember that there are no mistakes in the Universe and your greatest challenges represent your greatest growth opportunities. Therefore, your enemies and your challenges are the best things that could happen to you. Send only loving energy to your adversaries.

37. CHEER FOR THE OPPOSING TEAM.

What would it take for you to be happy when the other team scores a basket? Think about how good it feels when you get what you want. It feels the same when someone else gets what they want. Wish that feeling on other people.

38. SING LOUDER THAN ANYONE ELSE.

Set an example for the people around you. If you sing loudly, others will follow suit. There is nothing more inspiring than an entire stadium singing at the top of its lungs.

39. ACKNOWLEDGE SOMEONE AT LEAST ONCE A DAY.

This is a form of gratitude and it makes the other person feel really good. People love to know when they have made a difference in your life. Tell them. It is especially important to acknowledge your children, your partner and your parents.

40. SAY GRACE OR BE THANKFUL BEFORE EVERY MEAL.

Hold hands. Take a moment to be present to the gratitude you feel for being fortunate to have food to eat. Bless the earth for providing the food. Hold the vision that it is possible for everyone on Earth to get what they need.

41. LEAD BY EXAMPLE.

Be the first to do something. Use actions, not words. Be positive and encouraging. Allow others to follow in their own way.

42. SMILE.

It's a gift you can give for free. It is a great way to exercise your face. Look people in the eye when you smile at them. Smile with your whole body.

> *"We cannot hold a torch to light another's path without brightening our own."*
>
> —Ben Sweetland

appendix

BOOK CLUB DISCUSSIONS

This section is intended to support your book club while you are reading this book. Book clubs are a fantastic forum for discussion and expansion when studying new ideas. This guide is intended to help make the materials more relevant for you at a personal level. I have included thought-provoking discussion points along with the opportunity for live book club teleconferences.

Below you will find all the resources you need for a successful book club meeting. A book club usually has a format that includes an introduction of the book, some information about the author and then an open group discussion of the book. There are also opportunities to participate in live conference calls with the author. Visit www.GinaML.com for more information.

Book Club Meeting Format

Introduction to The Secret of Successful Failing

The first thing that is different about this book is it is built on the contrarian viewpoint that *FAILURE is a good*

thing. This book teaches that failure is the key to under-standing what stands between you and what you really want. Everything you have ever believed about failure is false. The answers to all of your questions about your life are sitting right in front of you. Everything you experience is just a reflection of what is going on inside you. Your life is one great big mirror. If you want to see a different reflection, you will have to change yourself first. Your failures provide you the opportunity to see what is really there.

By understanding and using the lessons that come with NOT getting what you want, you will be able to have joy, power and happiness. The Law of Attraction states that we get what we attract—nothing more, nothing less. If you have something in your life that you don't want, you have attracted it. It simply cannot be any other way. The good news is that you can learn to attract anything you want into your life. Anything!

We have been conditioned to believe that happiness is dependent on getting something—but this is an outright lie. Happiness is a choice we make and has nothing to do with getting anything. If you are not happy, you have chosen it that way. It didn't "happen" to you. True, it hurts to fail. The problem is we have been brainwashed into thinking that it is more painful to fail than to give up all our hopes and dreams. Instead, let's be responsible for our own happiness and be accountable for what we attract so that we can live the joyful, powerful lives we were meant to live.

NOT getting something is like a road sign from the Universe that says, "Wrong way." By using your own life as a mirror and your results as feedback, you can direct your life in virtually any direction you want. NOT getting what you want is exactly what you need to live the life of your dreams!

About the Author of The Secret of Successful Failing

Gina Mollicone-Long has spent the last 15 years trailblazing new paths for the modern female entrepreneur. Her breadth of business experience ranges from big corporate to start-from-scratch entrepreneur; from high-tech to not-for-profit. In each and every endeavour, personal or professional, Gina brings her ferocious energy and her firm belief that the "impossible" is always possible.

Gina lives her beliefs. Her outside-the-mold career started with an Honours Engineering degree from the University of Toronto. Interestingly, Gina draws on the experience of her undergraduate thesis in Process Control Engineering to create a model called the "Feedback Loop of Life," which describes life as a simple process.

From there came a non-linear leap to the corporate world, in brand management roles at two large multinational corporations. These experiences were key in laying the foundation for a very solid mastery of marketing and advertising.

Next was a senior strategic role within a high-tech youth-inspired venture capital firm. Here, Gina worked in a

fast-paced environment to help channel passion into entre-
preneurial technology businesses and learned from the pros
how to launch a new venture and pique investor interest.

Her extensive work with non-profits includes many
volunteer positions on boards and committees as well
the leadership of a non-profit organization dedicated to
empowering girls and women.

Gina's attention, focus and energy have almost always
been directed at empowering girls and women. She has been
a speaker, trainer and motivator of girls and women, creating conferences and delivering keynote addresses. She has
been sought-out by the media for her opinion on women's
issues and she continues to be a strong advocate for girls
and women. She has been a Big Sister since 1997.

She manages all of this while being mom to her energetic children, Molly and Simon, and at the same time
helping to run the two other multi-national companies she
started with her husband, Andrew, in 2000. Their Fortune
500 clients include The Body Shop, Microsoft and KPMG,
among many others.

Through personal experiences, Gina is an expert on
getting unstuck and being fearless. For instance, she managed to get her self-described "anti-runner's" body over the
finish line at the Nike Women's Marathon in San Francisco
in an effort to move the impossible into possible. She also
liberated a long-time fear of heights by plummeting earth-
ward in one of the highest bungee jumps in the world.

There is no straight line with Gina; all her varied experiences have shaped her unique perspective as an
entrepreneur, speaker and human being. Being in Gina's
presence is to feel the unstoppable force of her passion,
excitement and most of all her ardent belief that others
can achieve their "impossible" too.

Open Group Discussion
This is an opportunity for each member of your group
to share her or his overall reaction to the book.

Discussion Points for The Secret of Successful Failing
1. Using the mirror principle to identify your passion:
   - What circumstances in your life currently reflect
     things that you care about?
   - What circumstances in your life currently reflect
     things that upset you?
   - What insight do you have about these reflections?
2. Identifying your fears:
   - Make a list of your fears.
   - Compare this list with others.
   - What similarities are there between your list
     and someone else's?
   - Choose one fear you would like to acknowledge
     and make peace with.
   - Discuss with the group or a partner how you
     plan to free yourself of this fear.

3. Taking the "im" out of imPOSSIBLE *now*:
   - Make a list of everything you consider to be imPOSSIBLE.
   - Choose one thing on the list and commit to making it POSSIBLE.
   - Share this and your ideas about how to make it happen with your group.
4. What gets YOUR attention?
   - What makes you happy?
   - What makes you cry?
   - What makes you angry?
   - What makes you frightened?
5. What other things help raise your energy?
   - Discuss other techniques for uplifting your spirit and maintaining a positive outlook.
6. What other things do NOT help raise your energy?
   - Discuss other things that keep you down.
   - What can you do to overcome them?
7. How to create a Powerpod:
   - Make a list of inspiring people who share your outlook on life.
   - Invite them to join your Powerpod.
   - Determine a regular meeting schedule and code of conduct for your group.
   - Consider that your book group is already a natural Powerpod. Would it work to expand your relationships?

Follow-Up and Supporting Materials

1. Templates for the 42-day project:
   - Download the templates and supporting documents for your own 42-day project at www.GinaML.com.
   - Consider working on a collective group project with your book group.
2. Templates for creating a Powerpod can be found at www.GinaML.com.
3. List of supporting downloads, links and call schedules:
   - If you are interested in having your club be part of a virtual book tour whereby you can interact directly with the author, visit www.GinaML.com and follow the links for book club support.

"Never walk away from failure. On the contrary, study it carefully—and imaginatively—for its hidden assets."
—Michael Korda

"There can be no real freedom without the freedom to fail."
—Erich Fromm

"A fall from the third floor hurts as much as a fall from the hundredth. If I have to fall, may it be from a high place."
—Paulo Coelho

SPECIAL BONUS OFFER

YOUR REGISTRATION IN THE
SUCCESSFUL FAILING TELESEMINAR
ABSOLUTELY FREE!

To reserve your spot*, please register immediately at

www.SuccessfulFailing.com

In the Successful Failing Teleseminar you will learn:

- Three simple questions to ask every time you are faced with a failure.
- A step-by-step process for using the Mirror Principle.
- How to master the Feedback Loop of Life.
- The secret to being free of your fear.
- How to overcome your obstacles.
- The common traits of all leaders.

By the end of the course, you will be able to turn every single failure into a positive experience. You will be more empowered in all of the moments of your life because you will understand how they serve you, even if they are difficult. You will finally be free to choose happiness as a way of being instead of waiting for it to happen to you. This course will change your life.

Register now at www.SuccessfulFailing.com or call 1-866-939-GINA

*This offer is open to all purchasers of *The Secret of Successful Failing* by Gina Mollicone-Long. Original proof of purchase is required. Group purchasers including corporations and/or organizations may not use one book to register more than one person. The offer is limited to the Successful Failing Teleseminar and registration in the seminar is subject to availability of spaces and/or changes to the program schedule. The value of this course is $300, as of April 2007. While participants will be responsible for their regular long-distance charges to the teleseminar phone number, admission to the teleseminar is complimentary. Participants are under no additional financial obligation whatsoever to Goddess Concepts or Gina Mollicone-Long. Goddess Concepts reserves the right to refuse admission and/or remove from the teleseminar anyone it believes is disrupting the seminar.

Reference #:

Pathfinders Publishing has elected to print this title on 100% post-consumer recycled paper with the recycled portion processed chlorine free. As a result, we have saved the following resources:

- 79 mature trees
- 55 million BTUs of total energy
- 6,975 lbs of greenhouse gases
- 28,876 gallons of water
- 3,708 lbs of solid waste

Pathfinders Publishing is a member of Green Press Initiative, a nonprofit program dedicated to supporting publishers in their efforts to reduce their use of fiber sourced from endangered forests. For more information, visit www.greenpressinitiative.org (eco savings calculation courtesy of www.papercalculator.org).

Caring for the Earth is up to us...

Show you care, plant a tree!

www.PlantATreeUSA.com

When prompted, enter eco-code: PATHFINDERS

CANADA ORDER FORM

(SEE REVERSE FOR USA)

Pathfinders Publishing
36 Toronto Street, Suite 850
Toronto, Ontario, Canada, M5C 2C5
PH: (877) 901-9298 • FAX: (905) 844-8153
www.pathpub.com • books@pathpub.com

3 Ways to Order:

Mail a copy of this form to the address above.
Fax this form to (905) 844-8153.
Email us at orders@pathpub.com.

ITEM (all prices in Canadian dollars)	Unit Cost	Qty.	Total
The Secret of Successful Failing	$23.95		
Shipping & Handling (per book)	$6.00		
GST	6%		
		Total	

Forms of payment:

Cheque: payable to Pathfinders Publishing.

Credit Card: ☐ VISA ☐ MasterCard ☐ Amex

Card # _____ Exp. Date _____

Name on card_____

Billing Address_____

City_____

Province _____

Postal Code _____

Ship to:

Name _____

Address_____

City_____

Province _____

Postal Code _____

USA ORDER FORM
(SEE REVERSE FOR CANADA)

))Pathfinders
)PUBLISHING

Pathfinders Publishing
999 3rd Avenue, Suite 3800
Seattle, WA 98104 USA
PH: (877) 901-9298 • FAX: (905) 844-8153
www.pathpub.com • books@pathpub.com

3 Ways to Order:

Mail a copy of this form to the address above.
Fax this form to (905) 844-8153.
Email us at orders@pathpub.com.

ITEM (all prices in USD)	Unit Cost	Qty.	Total
The Secret of Successful Failing	$19.95		
Shipping & Handling (per book)	$6.00		
		Total	

Forms of payment:

Check: payable to Pathfinders Publishing.

Credit Card: ☐ VISA   ☐ MasterCard   ☐ Amex

Card # _____ Exp. Date _____

Name on card_____

Billing Address_____

City _____

State _____

Zip Code_____

Ship to:

Name _____

Address_____

City_____

State _____

Zip Code_____